Training Retrievers
with Nigel Mann

A Cow for my dairy, a dog for my game
And a purse when a friend wants to borrow:
I'll envy no nabob his riches or fame
Or what honours may wait him tomorrow,
John Collins (1742–1808)

Training Retrievers
with Nigel Mann

compiled by
Michael F. Twist

SWAN·HILL
PRESS

Copyright © 2001 Nigel Mann & Michael F. Twist

Photography © Diana Ewings and Nigel Mann.
Drawings by Wendy Andrews.

First published in the UK in 2001
by Swan Hill Press, an imprint of Quiller Publishing Ltd.

British Library Cataloguing-in-Publication Data
 A catalogue record for this book
 is available from the British Library

ISBN 1 84037 279 6

Typeset by Phoenix Typesetting, Ilkley, West Yorkshire
Printed in England by St Edmundsbury Press, Bury St Edmunds, Suffolk.

Swan Hill Press
an imprint of Quiller Publishing Ltd
Wykey House, Wykey, Shrewsbury, SY4 1JA, England
Website:www.swanhillbooks.com

Foreword

Our lives often intersect in curious ways. Though I had long admired Nigel Mann's abilities with retrievers, it was not until the 1995 IGL Retriever Championship held on His Grace The Duke of Buccleuch's Queensberry Estate at Thornhill in Dumfriesshire that our paths crossed in any consequential way. Nigel was handling his yellow Labrador dog Lafayette Tolley, not yet a Field Trial Champion, on a first round retrieve and was struggling in the gloom to make his handling visible. I was nearby, camera in hand, and checking a pocket I was amazed to find that I had a pristine and neatly folded white handkerchief which I could present without embarrassment. The offer was readily accepted, the retrieve accomplished, and when Nigel sought to return my offering I encouraged him to hang on to it.

As the stake unfolded and Tolley responded with increasing resolve and style to everything asked of him, my interest in the outcome, which had a particular twist to it, became keener than ever. I found myself amused and strangely excited at the prospect that seemed to be unfolding. My handkerchief might actually win the Retriever Championship. The fantasy, sadly, remained just that. But the third place achieved by Nigel and Tolley was really admirable: so much so that I entertained no thought of reclaiming that white handkerchief.

Nigel first qualified for the Retriever Championship in 1969 and qualified again in 1971, 1992, 1995 and 1997, and on each occasion he has been in the awards. In 1999 he judged the Blue Riband event. Clearly, he has been doing something right. And now, with Michael Twist as his trusty scribe, he is sharing those ideas which have been effective with Springers and Goldens as well as Labradors.

Anyone familiar with my own writings over two decades and more will not be surprised if I say that I cannot agree with everything he says. I made a dog up to FT Ch without ever kennelling it, for instance. But not agreeing with everything is what makes you think. And, more than anything else, that is what matters. Nigel Mann's approach is bound to be helpful to anyone who wants to have a well-behaved gundog.

Nigel's success with Labradors did not stop him being enthusiastically thrilled by the Golden he acquired in 1997. He has an open mind, an approach to gundog training which manifestly gets results and, finally, an endless patience: and that's what makes it all possible. He doesn't mind how long he takes to get the results he's looking for. Hasten slowly as you read these thoughts.

Graham Cox

Contents

6 Introduction to Gunfire   43
The title of this chapter summarizes its contents. Read carefully before introducing to gunfire, progress with care, develop a train of thought – that a shot
equals a possible retrieve.

7 Developing Memory and Straight Running   47
You have been developing *instant* reaction since puppyhood. Now the time
between *seeing* and actually *retrieving* has to be increased. Lengthen distance of
run-backs, without loosing his interest in the retrieve. Utilize modern farming
methods to develop memory and straight running. Increase time, distance and
add the occasional diversion as progress.

8 Introduction to Fur and Feather   53
At nine to twelve months attach wings, pheasant or duck, to dummy with elastic
bands. Before retrieving let him sniff and hold it. How to overcome picking
feather if a problem. Treatment of rabbit skins for dummies. Introduction to
cold game by first putting the retrieve in nylon stockings or tights. A whole bird
tastes and smells totally different to a winged dummy. When retrieving well,
dispense with nylon. Start working from light cover.

9 Retrieving Over Jumps   58
No serious jumping until around one year. A jumping lane is a great help and
can be constructed in the garden. Introduce to each type of fence separately.
Once proficient in the 'lane' take him out into the country, working him over
as great a variety of jumps as you can find.

10 Hunting for and Retrieving Blinds   63
The time to learn to use his nose. Choose initial training site with care, where
he has to hunt within an area. *Always* work into the wind and make sure he
always has a retrieve. As he learns to use his nose, the retrieves become progressively harder. Ways of scenting dummies. When proficient on dummies
change to cold game and should he have problems start to handle onto the
'fall'.

11 Introduction to Water   68
As mentioned in a previous chapter, from an early age, let your pup splash
through puddles when out for a walk – again so the unusual becomes the usual.
Never put a puppy on a lead and drag him into water. Inspire confidence, wade in if
necessary. When he is frolicking around in the shallows, start giving short
retrieves. From day one putting down a retrieve is absolutely *taboo*. Then
develop exercise as described.

12 Taking a Runner
Many dogs will eventually learn to take the line of a runner on their own. That can take time, so this chapter is devoted to the various ways of developing what is a natural instinct and outlines ways of achieving this.

13 Long Retrieves – the Dummy Launcher
Dummy launchers can be a useful aid, but should be used *sparingly* with a young dog; they can easily hot up a youngster. However, if training on your own they have their uses, particularly for a marked retrieve across water, over a belt of trees, or putting a 'blind' out before starting a training session. A launcher has other uses, as described, in developing steadiness.

14 Steadiness to Fur and Live Game
If you've done your job correctly, steadiness to all artificial diversions should have become second nature, so now is the time to meet the real thing. In the country rabbits normally abound, making it easy to instill into his mind, from an early age, that they are taboo. The alternative is to find a trainer with a rabbit pen. Live game is more difficult, but several suggestions are offered.

15 The Moment of Truth
Pigeons, to date, have been banned, but now have a place in the training schedule. If you have access to a wood where you can shoot them coming into roost. Sit Jack about ten yards from you. Don't let him have more than two retrieves and be certain to clear his mouth of feathers *immediately*. A few such evenings will help put the finishing touches to your months of work. His first day out on a driven shoot he should be there as a *spectator*, after that develop his participation as advised, but slowly and with care.

16 So, the Shooting Season is Over
February is a time when both Guns and dogs can suffer withdrawal symptoms, but equally time to take stock of your training achievements and think about improvements. The Working Test season will soon be starting. You might well enjoy watching Tests, pick up a few tips and even consider having a run. But remember successful Test dogs are sharper on the whistle and look for pinpoint directions – so, should you become involved, remember that next season you will expect Jack to 'do his own thing' once in the area of a fall.

Nigel Mann (right) talking to his 'ghost' writer and friend Michael Twist.

Introduction

It was not until the end of the 1998/1999 shooting season that a chance remark, at the end of a field trial at which I was judging, sowed the seed that perhaps I might write a book on Retriever training. The idea was appealing, but I knew in my heart of hearts that a pen was unlikely to be as responsive to my requirements as the dogs I have trained are to my whistle. I may have been blessed with small amount of talent when it comes to training, for which I am truly grateful and to which I am continually adding, but I knew that, attractive though the suggestion was, writing is just not my forte.

The remark that actually led to this momentary flight of fancy was from a friend, who commented on the fact that I must be in a somewhat unique position, for the only five dogs of workable age in my small kennel had all won a field trial. One was a field trial champion, the other four had been first in novice stakes. Further, he laughingly said, if I didn't actually write a book, at least I should compile a training manual.

Some weeks later I was talking to a good friend, Michael Twist, an 'A' Panel field trial judge since 1963, with whom I have judged on a number of occasions, and who is also an author, with five books published, together with numerous articles on all aspects of field sports. During the course of our conversation he also suggested that I should write a book. I explained that, to be honest, whilst I could talk for hours about training and its various facets, committing these ideas to paper was quite another matter. He looked at me for a moment or two, smiled and said, 'Right, you talk and I'll write, but it will be your book, your training programme, not mine. I will just be the scribe.' I should explain that Michael wrote a book that has now gone into a second edition, *The Complete Guide To The Golden Retriever*, way back in 1988, exactly half of which is devoted to training. At one stage he and his wife, Cynthia, had three dogs in their kennel, all champions in the show ring and all open stake winners. So here was an offer I could not refuse – someone who could string a few words together, but also understood about training. That is how this book has come about. From the start he was adamant that his only contribution would be committing my ideas and theories to paper. However, he did agree that, where applicable, he would add the odd quote or two, or a reference to other works which might be appropriate, and explain the intricacies of the BVA/KC schemes. In spite of my attempts to persuade him otherwise he has stuck rigidly to this.

I first became interested in Labradors in 1956, after reading Peter Moxon's articles on training gundogs in the *Shooting Times*. Being very keen on shooting I was able to appreciate the merit of having a dog which was disciplined, but happy and anxious to please. This led to my buying a yellow Labrador bitch puppy, Floss, Peter Moxon's book, and a whistle, and commencing training. I followed Peter Moxon's instructions to the letter and was careful not to be tempted to cut corners or rush things. When I finally closed the book I was more than happy with the outcome. Floss turned out to be an excellent gamefinder and a great shooting companion, who consistently proved that she had learned her lessons well. In fact I was so pleased with her that the following season I entered her in a field trial. Much to my delight she was awarded a Certificate of Merit and I came away feeling I had done a reasonably good job at my first attempt, so much so that I bought another yellow bitch puppy and trained her on to become a really good and responsive gundog, from whose work I got much pleasure.

In 1968 I did something which would horrify the trialling purists of today, but which also demonstrates the vast gulf that has developed between the show-bred Labradors and those bred purely for work. I purchased a young yellow bitch, Goldofer Blondie, born on 24 May 1965, who was entirely what today would be classified as show-bred. She was by Ch Rookwood Peter Gold, out of Brentchase Crinoline. I quickly realised that she had a lot of potential and set about training her to the highest standard I could achieve, which I hoped would be sufficient to warrant entering her in field trials. Blondie proved to be an outstanding gamefinder. Armed with this knowledge, and having enjoyed my brief but most pleasurable sortie into the world of field trialling, I decided to run her in a few stakes.

It is difficult, even now, to express my total elation when I quickly made her up as a field trial champion and qualified her for the 1969 Retriever Championship, being awarded a Diploma of Merit. In 1971 Blondie again qualified for the Retriever Championship. Much to my surprise, and that of most of the spectators, she was placed second – everyone seemed to think she had won comfortably. I left for home with mixed feelings. First, whilst disappointed at not winning, I was thrilled at coming second. Secondly, I wondered whether, if I had had my hair cut, I would have won. I was young and, like many men of my age around that time, my hair was shoulder-length. After the presentation and speeches were over, one of the judges, a senior member of the Kennel Club Field Trial Committee, came up to me and said, 'Young man, if you are going to continue field trialling, get your hair cut', and walked away. Shortly after that I had a very serious illness, which resulted in my having to retire from both shooting and field trialling for a number of years, to the extent that I put all thoughts of ever running a dog again behind me.

In 1985 my wife went off and, unbeknown to me, bought a Springer Spaniel puppy, Anne of Keswick – pet name Sal. This rekindled my interest in dogs and, when Sal was old enough, out came Peter Moxon's book and all the love and fervour for training was reawakened. Sal never ran in a trial, but I won a number of working tests with her.

In 1987 I went to look at a litter of Labradors and came away with a bitch puppy, Black Purdey of Keswick. She turned out to be an excellent buy, trained on well and proved to be an outstanding gamefinder. Not only did she fulfil my requirements in this respect, she won a two-day open stake, qualifying her for the 1992 Retriever Championship. It was exhilarating to be back in the 'big time', and I set off for Sandringham, where the Championship was being hosted by Her Majesty, full of anticipation and with my hair cut! I was not disappointed. No third or fourth were awarded, only first and second and four Diplomas of Merit – one of which went to Purdey.

In due course Purdey was mated to FT Ch Kilderkin Renoir and produced a lovely litter, out of which I kept a yellow dog, Lafayette Tolley. As he matured Tolley fulfilled all my hopes (well nearly all, we would always like a little bit more), first as a gamefinder and then as a possible field trialler. In 1994 I entered him in a novice stake, his first trial, which he won. The following year, 1995, he won a two-day open stake, qualifying him for the Retriever Championship, in which he came third. In 1997 I won again with Tolley, making him a FT champion and, of course, qualifying for the Retriever Championship; this time he came fourth. It was gratifying that he was the only one in the awards bred and handled by his owner. I have been fortunate that so far, on each occasion I have run in the Retriever Championship, I have been in the awards. But with so many top-class dogs competing there always has to be an element of luck. Tolley has won numerous working tests, including coming first in the prestigious *Shooting Times* Gundog Weekend in 1995.

In the autumn of 1997 I added a Golden Retriever dog puppy to my kennel, Canburne Fennel of Lafayette – pet name Kes. I was interested to find out if it was the case that, on a bad scenting day, Goldens took an 'air scent', and further, whether what the great Eric Baldwin frequently said was true, namely that a good Golden, well trained, was a joy to handle. I obviously cannot comment on the training, but I have on numerous occasions found that Kes, when scent was poor, was able to pick retrieves with comparative ease, whereas my Labradors struggled. I ran him in a novice stake for the first time in January 1999, and he won. He made his first appearance in an open working test later in the year and was placed first. As recently as April 2000 he was leading individual dog out of ten teams of five, taking part in the Windsor Great Park Test, dropping only 6 marks out of a possible 140. So, to date, I am well pleased with my Golden. At the 1999 Retriever Championship I had the honour of being one of the judges.

I am well aware that there will be those who will not agree with my approach to training. Many will say I start too soon, but I feel a puppy is never too young to learn. Yes, it takes time, but I think it is time well spent. Others will probably say my methods take too long. Fair enough, we all have our own ideas. I enjoy my dogs; I am not a professional trainer, but the modicum of success I have achieved is an indication that I must be doing something right. First and foremost I want a dog to find game and be under control, and to achieve this I believe one must 'hasten slowly'.

To anyone who may buy this book I say, first, that I hope it will be of help and, secondly, that I trust your dog fulfils all your expectations and that you are rewarded, for all your patience and hard work, with a dog that is a true companion when out shooting.

Chapter 1

Points to Consider before Buying a Puppy

The majority of people who decide to become the owner of a Retriever puppy which they hope will one day be a gundog and probably a constant companion as well, will have preconceived ideas as to which breed they prefer. Labradors predominate, at least as far as Kennel Club registrations are concerned. The most recent figures available at the time of writing, those for 1997, show that 34,788 Labradors were registered, 15,214 Golden Retrievers, 1,502 Flat-Coated Retrievers, 140 Curly-Coated Retrievers, 72 Chesapeake Bay and 50 Nova Scotia Duck Tolling Retrievers. The last three breeds, whilst they are undoubtedly very nice dogs, are seldom seen in the shooting field today. Flat-Coats, back in the twenties and thirties, were very much the gamekeepers' dog, tough and hard-working. Indeed, they still are, but they have a will of their own and are not the easiest to train.

The choice is really between Labradors and Golden Retrievers. There are of course other categories of gundogs that retrieve, but this book is confined to those classified by the Kennel Club as 'Retrievers'. The Labrador as we know the breed today, although changed in type, first appeared in the shooting field around 1890, but several decades passed before they started to oust the Flat-Coats from their privileged position, not only as the gamekeepers' first choice but also that of the landed gentry. At the beginning of the century Retrievers were, as far as registration with the Kennel Club was concerned, a bit of a mishmash, for whilst the origins of Golden Retrievers and Labradors were entirely different, it appears that Yellow Labradors and Golden Retrievers were registered together under the heading of 'Retrievers (Golden or Yellow)', in spite of the fact that the Golden Retriever Club was formed in 1913 and they were recognised as a separate breed. It was around 1908 that Goldens were first exhibited at shows, and they made their first appearance in field trials in either 1910 or 1911. Surprisingly, according to information obtained from the Kennel Club it was not until 1916 that the Labrador Club was formed.

All that is history, and both breeds have gone their separate ways, both producing top-class gundogs. So it comes down really to two main factors – personal preference and faith in one's ability to train a gundog. Ask yourself what you want a Retriever for. The answer has to be to find runners and to retrieve game you cannot pick yourself, irrespective of what breed takes your fancy. Exactly! So, when choosing the parents of your future shooting companion, never put steadiness and style ahead of nose, stamina, keenness to hunt and game-finding ability.

It is probable that Goldens are softer than Labradors, not in facing cover – far from it – but when it comes to training. They are by nature both soft and affectionate. The late Eric Baldwin (owner of the famous Palgrave gundogs, who made up five Labradors and five Goldens as FT champions, plus breeding a number more) once wrote:

I have been asked many times why we do not see more Goldens in professional hands. I have put this question to several great trainers, but have never received the same answer. Could it be that Goldens are more affectionate, so giving the outward appearance of softness, that they mature more slowly, or is it because of the time it takes at the end of a day's work to clean the long hair of burrs and the feet of balls of mud? Make no mistake a well-trained Golden Retriever from good working stock is very difficult to beat in competition. Goldens have excellent scenting powers and usually come into their own on a bad scenting day.

A great professional trainer, who had made up a number of Labradors as FT champions, once said to Eric Baldwin, 'I don't understand why you waste time with those Golden things, they're too soft for my way of training.' He was very good at his job and produced several winners of the Retriever Championship, but he was noted for his tough training methods. Another trainer of the fifties and sixties, Jim Cranston, whom Eric Baldwin described as the most complete dog trainer he ever met, always declared that a Golden, once it knew what was wanted, would give 100 per cent, whilst other breeds would 'retain' 5–10 per cent. If you have not made up your mind, visit a few kennels or trainers; most will be ready to advise, but, at this stage, just listen to what they have to say. Do not get talked into buying a puppy until you have gone away and thought through what you have learned.

Fifty years ago buying a gundog puppy was a comparatively simple operation. You found a litter you liked and then it was a case of 'yer pays yer money an' yer takes yer choice'. All forms of livestock, unless specifically stated otherwise, were sold on the then accepted basis of *caveat emptor*, 'let the buyer beware', and the chances were that, in law, if something went wrong, this would apply. However, over the years things have changed to such a degree that it becomes essential to outline briefly how the schemes now emanating from both the Kennel Club and the British Veterinary Association could mislead the uninitiated when embarking on what should be a comparatively easy and enjoyable process – namely the purchase of a puppy to train on as a gundog and shooting companion.

First, let us look at the BVA/KC Inherited Eye Diseases Scheme, which came into being in the early sixties and was, and indeed still is, well supported by the breeders of Golden Retrievers, Labradors and many other breeds. There had for several years prior to this been a major problem in Irish Setters with generalised progressive retinal atrophy (PRA), which led to defective vision, at the time often referred to as night blindness and subsequently bringing about total blindness. This caused considerable concern about what might be happening in other breeds, not just gundogs. A scheme was set up whereby breeders could have their dogs examined, annually if they so wished, under the BVA/KC Eye Scheme and certified free from hereditary eye diseases.

In the case of both Goldens and Labradors the two main worries were central PRA (not generalised as in the case of Irish Setters) and hereditary cataract (HC). Central PRA, whilst very serious, leads to a state of peripheral vision rather than central, and does not inevitably bring about total blindness like generalised PRA. Fortunately, regular testing and not breeding from affected stock has all but eliminated this problem. In the case of HC, whilst the incidence of this has been vastly reduced since the scheme began, it can still crop up most unexpectedly. For example, a young Golden Retriever dog whose parents had up-to-date clear certificates, when being presented for his second examination, was failed for having HC. However, not only did his parents have clear certificates, but so did all his grandparents and great grandparents, together with a large majority of the next generation. This is by no means an isolated case, for there have been many, many more in both Labradors and Goldens, and indeed in other breeds, where a puppy bred from parents having BVA/KC certificates of freedom from hereditary eye diseases has been failed. Such certificates are an indication that the breeder has done all that he or she can in this respect, but they do not constitute a warranty.

When assessing the value of such certificates, in respect of a puppy intended to become one's shooting companion (not as a future brood bitch or potential stud dog), they must be viewed in the right perspective. All aspects must be carefully considered, bearing in mind that 75–80 per cent of all puppies bred by even the most conscientious and well-known breeders finish up as companions of one kind or another and almost certainly will never meet an ophthalmologist throughout their lifetime, nor indeed a radiologist, and will live long and happy lives, free of lameness and with no obvious eye defects. Over a period of some thirty-five years or more, whilst everything possible has been done to eradicate hereditary eye diseases, the fact remains that this has not been fully achieved. One has to ask oneself the question, 'Why should it have?' After all if it were possible in dogs, why has it not been achieved in humans?

The mention of radiologists leads us into the next consideration – hip dysplasia. The BVA/KC Hip Dysplasia Scheme came into being about 1960, when major problems were occurring in German Shepherd Dogs. The scheme was open to all breeds, but as one of the first scrutineers of the X-rays submitted, a highly respected veterinary surgeon, the late John Dall, was heard to say on numerous occasions that it was, in his opinion, a non-starter from its inception, for three reasons. First, it was based on the assumption that the hip structure and movement of all breeds was the same, which he was adamant was not the case, his favourite comparison being between a Bulldog and a Greyhound. Secondly, the initial scheme supplied insufficient data to be of any great help to breeders. Mating a dog and a bitch which in the early days would have been described as having hips 'within the standard of normality' was absolutely no guarantee that the progeny would have similar hips. Thirdly, when dogs were failed under the scheme no indication was given as to how bad the hips really were, and therefore only a very small percentage of breeders gave cognisance to the scheme.

It was not until around 1978, thanks to the persistence and hard work of the geneticist Dr Malcolm Willis, that the BVA/German Shepherd League (GSDL) hip-scoring scheme came into being, which was extended to other breeds in 1983. This proved to be far more enlightening, with hips scored from 0 to 108, 54 for each hip. The lower the score the better. However, it quickly exposed an anomaly, for it was said that 0–4 was the equivalent of what had been described as 'within the standard of normality' and scores of 5–8 were the equivalent of what was known as 'a breeder's letter'. After some sixteen years of hip scoring one is left wondering from what source, and indeed on what basis, the BVA/KC conjured up a standard which they claimed to be 'normality', which is said to be equal to a score of 0–4.

Until 30 January 1998, under the BVA/KC Hip Dysplasia Scheme 26,401 Labradors had been scored, varying from 0 to 104 and having a mean score of 16. Over the same period 18,875 Golden Retrievers were scored from 0 to 106, with a mean score of 20. Of the numerically smaller breeds 2,753 Flat-Coated Retrievers were scored, ranging from 0 to 85, mean score 9. There have also been 164 Curly-Coated Retrievers scored, ranging from 1 to 59 with a mean score of 11 and, finally, X-rays for 93 Nova Scotia Duck Tolling Retrievers have been submitted, scoring 0 to 63, with a mean score of 15. These figures relate to all the dogs in these breeds whose X-rays have been sent forward for reading under the scheme since 1983.

When one relates these figures, over a period of fifteen years, to the overall population in the country of the two most popular breeds of Retrievers, which must, at a most conservative figure, be around 150,000 Goldens and probably at least double that number of Labradors, one is left wondering about the value of a scheme which encompasses such a relatively small percentage. As I have said, 80 per cent of the puppies breeders sell will go as companions, be they pets or gundogs, and the majority will live carefree lives, unlikely to suffer from serious lameness due to a hereditary cause.

Over a number of years Dr Willis, when talking about hip dysplasia, would state that when assessing the breeding potential of a dog, he placed hips about fourth in his requirements. Certainly as far as Golden Retrievers are concerned it seems to be a 'no win' situation, for after the first three years 3,456 X-rays had been scrutinised, with a mean score of 18.47. Up to 14 February 1998 17,462 had been seen and the mean score had risen to 19.60. A minimal score would be a pleasing attribute to one's gundog, but unless one is involved commercially, i.e. breeding deliberately to sell, providing a dog is sound it does not really matter what the score is, for there are a large number of dogs which could have, or indeed are known to have, high scores, but fulfil their job as a hard-working gundog and never have a day's lameness throughout their working life. Not always, but in a very large number of cases, should a dog become lame from hip dysplasia, a comparatively simple muscle-cutting operation, known as a pectineus resection, followed by three to four months of controlled exercise, will leave the dog able to lead a full and normal life. Alternatively, in very bad cases, another operation, excision arthroplasty, which is basically removing the head of the femur, has been highly successful. If you are very wealthy you can even arrange for your dog to have a hip replacement operation similar to that regularly performed on humans!

Whether they have changed their approach, I do not know, but for many years the Guide Dogs for the Blind Association did not make hips a major issue in their breeding policy, any more than at least one county's police force did when recruiting dogs. In the latter case a veterinary surgeon X-rayed them and had to state whether he considered the dogs capable of working up to the age of eight. When deliberating on the importance of hip scores, pause to think. First, mating a dog with a very low score to a bitch of an equal standard is no guarantee of breeding progeny that have correspondingly low-scoring hips. These are normally not X-rayed until they are at least twelve months old. Secondly, there can be a quite amazing variation in the scores of litter brothers and sisters – a clear indication that management after puppies are sold and go to a new environment can have a major effect on the outcome if they are scored. Even an injury at birth, according to some vets, can bring about a disproportional score.

One factor I have not yet mentioned is that both the eye and hip schemes are voluntary. Therefore, if a breeder or owner has a dog X-rayed and sees that the score is going to be high, then he or she will frequently decide not to pursue the matter further, for it costs around £21 to be officially scored. I referred earlier to breeding with the main objective of having puppies to sell – a perfectly legitimate thing to do – which does not categorise the breeder as a puppy farmer, for the cost of maintaining even a small kennel these days is high. If this is the case then it might be wise to have the eyes and hips done under the BVA/KC schemes. However, whatever the results, bear in mind that any certificates you may receive do not constitute a warranty; they are, according to the BVA, merely an opinion. Therefore, since we live in a time of almost instant litigation, should anything go wrong and a puppy becomes the centre of a legal dispute, it might well be worth while giving a little thought to a 'condition of sale' document, for no longer does the old adage of *caveat emptor* apply. Any such case would be dealt with under the Sale of Goods Act, which means, as the law stands at the time of writing, that a puppy, or any other living creature, is treated as an inanimate object, being categorised in the same way as a faulty washing machine or electric stove. Appendix I gives an example of such a 'condition of sale', but it must be stressed that this is for reference only and should be adapted to suit individual requirements. Anyone who is seeking to use such a document should first take legal advice. To most people this will seem to be an unnecessary precaution, but such a document leaves everyone concerned knowing where they stand. One other word of advice: if a sale was made using BVA/KC certificates and, in due course, a puppy did not fulfil the expectations that a buyer might reasonably anticipate from documents relating to the parents of the puppy, then a court of law might well find that there had been misrepresentation.

If all this has left you mystified by the inadequacies of the BVA and the KC, then have pity on those who have to cope with them year in, year out! If you are looking for a Retriever puppy that one day will pick your game, it frankly does not matter a great deal what the parents' hip scores are, as long as they are sound and are good workers. Much the same applies to minor eye problems. Most ophthalmologists agree that hereditary cataract only has a damaging effect in a very small percentage of those affected. Dogs, like humans, suffer from time to time from various ailments, and unless this obsession with hips and eyes, which is becoming almost a cult with many breeders, particularly in the show world, is viewed in the right perspective, it will do more harm than good as far as the things that really matter in a gundog are concerned – i.e. temperament, nose (so important), stamina, keenness to hunt and game-finding ability.

Chapter 2

Choosing Your Puppy

So the BVA/KC schemes, whilst eminently worthy in their endeavours, do not take into serious consideration the makings of a good gundog. It is no good having a dog with zero/zero hips and clear eye certificates, if its temperament is such that it will amputate your finger if you go to touch it, flies at a dog should it come near it, or crunches up anything it is asked to retrieve. This, of course, is exaggerating the possible problems, but it is essential to have one's priorities in the right order, and heading the list should be the temperament of both parents of your puppy, coupled with their game-finding ability.

The next point that cannot be emphasised too strongly is that you should not be in a rush. You cannot buy a puppy like going to a supermarket and buying a tin of beans off the shelf. Perhaps this is not strictly accurate, for you probably could get one from a puppy farm, but how it would turn out is anybody's guess and this approach is certainly not advised. Of course there are exceptions to every rule, like the Golden Retriever puppy bought from a pet shop at the end of the sixties which eventually went Best of Breed at Crufts and laid the foundation for one of the top dual-purpose kennels in the country. But this is very rare.

If you happen to be a regular at a shoot where one of your fellow Guns has a bitch with outstanding game-finding ability and you learn that the owner is going to breed from her, you need look no further – a proviso being that he uses a stud dog of equal quality. Of course it may well be that one of the pickers-up at the shoot has a bitch that you have seen 'bringing home the bacon' time after time, a strong runner or a dead bird from the heaviest of cover – birds that could not be picked by hand. Such a bitch, bred to the right dog, could produce what you are wanting, so it is well worth waiting. Seeing is believing, and visual proof surpasses a fistful of certificates!

If you are not in the fortunate position of knowing of a bitch out of whom you would dearly love to have a puppy, then it is a case of scanning the advertisements in the *Shooting Times,* the *Shooting Gazette* and possibly *Horse and Hound.* Puppies advertised in the last publication largely seem to be from genuine working homes.

Whatever the source, the formula for selecting a puppy remains the same. There is little point in seeing them until they are five and a half to six weeks old. Prior to that, unless you possess a heart of stone, they are just loveable little creatures which spend their lives eating, sleeping and playing. There are those who have bred many litters who will tell you that, if you are selecting a puppy as a potential show dog, you should do so before it is forty-eight hours old and then, having made your selection, stick with it through the weeks that follow. Equally, there are breeders who, from a work point of view, will greatly favour a puppy that, in its early days, barges through to the milk bar, knocking its siblings out of the way. The belief is that it will be a hard-going dog in cover. However, unless you are actually breeding a litter yourself, these ideas are really irrelevant. Having found a litter whose parents fulfil your criteria, it is advisable to see them at least twice, if possible around five and a half to six

Choose a puppy with a broad head and dark intelligent eye.

weeks, and if you like what you have seen, again at eight weeks, which would be the normal age to finalise your choice and take the new member of your household home. However, there is much to consider before that. Normally kennel-reared puppies are more worldly-wise, providing the kennel has an outside run from which to view all that is going on in the vicinity. They will see birds, people passing, possibly cars coming and going, and in the summer time an initially terrifying monster called a lawn-mower passing up and down outside their run. All these things are largely missed by litters reared indoors, where frequently a few little yaps will have someone running to give them attention. Ideally, in the summer – and indeed in the winter providing it is not too cold – the litter should have been allowed to run out from the kennel, strictly supervised, on grass if possible. It is all part of learning – it cannot start too soon, however trivial.

When you go to see a litter, ask if they have been treated against roundworm. This should have been done first at three weeks and again at five. Even when a bitch has been correctly wormed before whelping, if she is not completely free, the eggs of the roundworm can be passed on to the puppies through the bitch's milk. By the time they are six weeks, if they are wormy, the puppies' coats will be starey and lack lustre, even if they are only moderately affected. However, if everything else pleases you, suggest to the owner that he or she worms the puppies and that if they then look better in their coats in a couple of weeks' time you will be interested in buying one.

Whether kennel- or house-reared, try to see the puppies out of doors at six weeks. Look for a puppy that is adventurous and comes if you call it, obviously not by name as it is most unlikely to have one, but to a call of 'pup, pup, pup' or something similar. Let them run around a bit more and then call them again, and as they come to you clap your hands as loud as you can. Alternatively, blow up a small paper bag and burst it when they are three or four yards away. Forget any that hightail it in the opposite direction, but those that come on, showing they are bold and not scared, are the ones to consider seriously.

Look for a puppy with a broad head, not a bull head which is coarse and too strong, and dark, intelligent eyes. The old song which goes 'How much is that doggy in the window, the one with the waggly tail?', whilst written as a sentimental ditty, also portrays something you should be looking for – an out-going personality, a puppy that wags its tail when you talk to it, indicating a happy and friendly nature. Look for good bone and check the ears for mites – not uncommon in puppies – particularly if the breeder is not greatly experienced. They are, however, easily got rid of.

Having made your selection, pick it up and ask for the remaining puppies to be returned to their kennel. Then put 'your' puppy down, play with it a bit, walk away, call it and let it know it's the greatest puppy that ever lived. Now comes the moment of truth. Knot up your handkerchief, restrain the pup with a hand around its chest (do not scruff it, which will upset it), show it your knotted handkerchief and throw it a few yards. Do not restrain the pup at all; let it go at once. If the retrieving instinct is there, and if you have chosen the right parents, your handkerchief will be 'retrieved'. It is a bonus if the pup comes straight back to you, although there is a strong possibility you may have to make a quick but gentle catch in the slips as it heads for home. You should have positioned yourself so you are between the 'retrieve' and the kennel as, at this stage, the puppy will be of the opinion that 'finders keepers'.

If you decide that you have found the puppy you want, then it is down to business. You require the Kennel Club registration certificate. The breeder may or may not have this; it all depends at what age the breeder sent in the application, and whether there were any queries. However, it is important to make sure that registration has been applied for, as it leads to extra work if it has not and you subsequently have to do it yourself. You should be given a five-generation pedigree, and many top breeders today supply copies of eye certificates and hip scores for the sire and dam. Remember, however, that these in no way constitute a guarantee. Unless you know the person with whom you are dealing, it is as well to have an endorsement on the receipt you should be given after payment that the KC registration certificate will be forwarded upon receipt.

When you collect your puppy try to arrange to have someone drive you if at all possible, so that the pup can travel on your knee. Apart from the fact that, for the puppy, it is a big wide world it is being launched into and human contact will help avert some of the fears to which it must inevitably be subject, it is the start of the bonding process which is so essential to developing the understanding and trust that must be forged between owner and dog. Also take an old cardigan or pullover for it to snuggle into, so that it becomes familiar with your scent.

Chapter 3

Early Days

Hopefully you will not have too long a journey before introducing your puppy to its new home – that strange new existence, in a puppy's mind, light years away from the reassuring company of its siblings, and all the familiar smells – remember, a puppy's olfactory powers are vastly superior to ours. When possible collect your pup as early in the day as can be arranged and let it travel home on your lap; that is, of course, if you can arrange for someone to drive you. Take an old cardigan, or pullover, for it to snuggle into, the sweatier the better, so that right from the start it becomes familiar with your scent.

Assuming that it is to live in a kennel, and that is the only sensible place if you are to have success in guiding your new acquisition along the road to becoming the gundog you secretly long to own – the one that will be at your heel when, in years to come, you walk around the corner of a wood and join your friends. One says, 'I know I've another cock down in those briars, we've tried all the dogs, but can't pick it. It probably ran.' Nonchalantly you say 'I may as well give my old lad a try.' A click of the fingers and he's off into the rough. You can hear him, but not see him, the cover's too thick, and then – presto, he's on the way back, the cock firmly, but gently, held, delivered safely to hand. From such dreams great gundogs are fashioned, but such dreams are a long way away and many hours of patient training lie ahead before they can be fulfilled – common sense decrees that you will already have the kennel fully prepared, ready for occupation. Ideally the sleeping quarters should be not less than 6 ft × 4 ft. The floor should be concrete, with a smooth finish, draining to the door, which can be easily cleaned. If you cannot build it yourself do not be so foolish as to buy a prefab kennel with a wooden floor. The latter can quickly become impregnated with urine and will stink – and it will continue to do so, however much you scrub it. Further, if the kennel smells, it will not be long before your dog does too, and that, in years to come, will win you no 'brownie points' if you are travelling to a shoot with friends! A raised wooden sleeping bed is a must. The kennel should be well ventilated and in a way that can be regulated. There should be an outside run, at least 8 ft × 6 ft, bigger if possible, with a concrete floor, and with a slight fall on it so that it drains easily. It should be fenced with chain-link to a height of at least 6 ft. Finally, if your pup's homecoming is in cold weather, you should fix up an infrared heater, approximately 3 ft above the puppy when lying down; it can be harmful if it is too close.

To return to the homecoming, here is a useful tip, unattractive though it may seem. If the puppies have been kennelled on newspaper, ask the breeder to have some that has recently been soiled and removed from the kennel ready for you in a plastic bag, which you can take home and spread on the floor of your kennel. Some will say, 'Disgusting!' No one is arguing, but to your pup – or let's give him a name, let's call him Jack – those dirty sheets of paper are a symbol of life as he has known it until just hours ago, when he was suddenly whisked away from the only world he knew. The smell is familiar, reassuring – one thing at least to which he can relate in his new surroundings.

When you have introduced Jack to his kennel, put your old cardigan, or whatever it was he lay on whilst on your knee in the car, into his sleeping quarters, even if you have a nice cosy vetbed, or a bed of straw for him, for he will already have begun to associate the smell with you. Stay with him for a little while whilst he explores, make a fuss of him – not too much, just keep using his name and occasionally stroking him to help him gain confidence. The sooner you establish the fact that you are his best friend, the easier your job will become. There will undoubtedly be those who will consider that such steps towards early bonding are nonsense, such as members of the 'chuck 'em in the kennel, treat 'em tough' school. Fortunately this is a school that is slowly becoming extinct. One can usually spot pupils from such an 'academy', even as adults, for their distrust is ever-apparent, frequently cringing and constantly casting apprehensive looks at their owner. Of course there has to be discipline, but that does not mean constant bullying. Never nag. If some 'straightening out' has to be done at a later date, which undoubtedly it will, then try and make it a one-off lesson.

But that is in the future. What has to be done at this age is to build up a really good rapport. Lesson number one is the constant use of his name – use it every time you are in contact with him, until the mere mention of his name makes his tail wag and he learns that he is Jack, the centre of attention.

So your pup is home and, providing he has had a sick-free journey (which he almost certainly will have if he was travelling on your lap – it could have been very different if he'd been left on his own in the back of your vehicle), he will probably be wanting something to eat. It is advisable, for the first day or two, to continue with the same food and routine he has been used to, before changing to your choice of the large selection of complete foods available. By the way, fresh water should *always* be available in the kennel, preferably in a bowl that cannot be turned over.

Like all products, complete foods vary enormously, some being much better than others. Beware of cheap brands with a high protein content – they are not always what they seem. Many concentrates, not just dog foods but also compounds prepared for farm livestock and horses, may, on paper, contain what appears to be the correct level of protein when analysed in a laboratory, but with no nutritional value. This is due to what are known in the trade as 'empty proteins'. Chief amongst these are feathers, not so much the quills as the fine hair-like filaments growing from these, known as vanes. They are ground up together to produce a substance that, when analysed, is shown to be high in protein, but in actual fact, as a source of food, is useless. Actually if you were to keep all your hair and nail trimmings, grind them and had the resulting powder analysed you would find that you too had produced an 'empty protein'. Fortunately, such products normally have a short life, for obvious reasons. Another source of what can be called 'partially empty protein' is vegetables. This food also looks good on paper, but they are frequently disappointing in relation to the condition and fitness of the dog.

There are of course many excellent complete dog foods on the market, but both Michael Twist and I have, for many years, used Skinners Dog Food (see Appendix II) with excellent results, producing champions both on the bench and in the field. There are those who are great believers in bullock's tripe as the main feed, but to produce a balanced diet carbohydrates should be fed as well. So, unless you have a big kennel and a good supply, it is easier and more beneficial to feed a well-balanced diet that has been carefully formulated, to cover the varying nutritional requirements for all age groups, from a recently weaned puppy upwards.

Up to the age of 5 or 6 months, four feeds a day are recommended, one of which should be milk, made up from milk powder that is of similar composition to that of a bitch's milk. Cow's milk is of little use to a puppy, for a bitch's milk contains approximately three times as much fat, double the amount of casein (the main protein present in milk) and somewhere between nine and ten times the amount of albumin (water-soluble protein) of that found in cow's milk. Cow's milk has total solids of approximately 12.92%, whereas for a bitch they are about 24.50%. There are a number of excellent brands of milk powder to choose from, but in my opinion it would be difficult to better Skinners.

Assuming you collected Jack at eight weeks, you should contact your veterinary surgeon with regard to immunisation against the various ailments from which dogs can suffer. There are those who pooh-pooh such precautions as unnecessary, particularly for a dog living in the country, on two grounds: first, that a dog will build up a natural immunity, and secondly, that the vast majority of responsible dog owners have, over many years, regularly vaccinated their dogs, thus greatly reducing the instances of such diseases throughout the country, and the risk of infection is thus less. But it would be unwise to gamble. Administration differs slightly according to the vaccine used, but normally the first 'jab' is at eight or nine weeks, and covers leptospirosis, parvovirosis and parainfluenza. This is a good time to get your vet to give him a 'once-over', for example for such things as ear nits, which are not uncommon in even the best-run kennel. However, in the case of the latter, the problem should have been noted and rectified before Jack came into your possession.

A second visit to the vet follows two weeks after the first. It does not matter if it is a few days late, but during that time any puppy should remain away from other dogs, other than those on its home territory, which I assume will have been fully vaccinated. The second injection covers distemper, hepatitis, leptospirosis, parvovirosis and parainfluenza. However, immunity is not achieved overnight and ten to fourteen days should elapse before you allow Jack to mix freely with other dogs. It should be said that in a very small number of cases – and it really is very small – some puppies do not respond to vaccination and, again very occasionally, one gets a hypersensitive reaction. In the most unlikely event of the latter happening it would be as well to contact your vet.

I am a great believer in getting the vet to come out to the car to give the 'shots'. There is little point in keeping a puppy isolated until it is fully vaccinated, if one takes it into a surgery, where, quite possibly, some of the patients waiting to see the vet have an infectious disease such as kennel cough. Some vets think that to ask them to come out to your car to give the injections is a slur on their establishment, but it is nothing of the sort. Having given the required 'shots' they are the first to tell you to keep Jack away from other dogs until the prescribed time has passed to establish immunity.

Right from the start, at every opportunity, take Jack out in the car – not for long tiring journeys, just short runs of a few miles. If you have a hatchback of one kind or another – and most shooting or 'doggy' people have – put him in the back and for the first few outings try to get someone to drive you, so that you can sit on the back seat and talk to him and reassure him. A great juggernaut thundering by or nearly sitting in the boot can be an alarming experience for one so young. However, it will not take long for him to become quite at home in any vehicle, once the initial nerves are conquered. The majority of youngsters enjoy the ride, particularly, once they've had their shots, if it leads to somewhere exciting where they are let out to have a run and explore.

During these early days it would be as well to buy a whistle; there are a variety on the market. However, I suggest you contact Turner Richards (see Appendix III), who can supply all your requirements, not only whistles but all the other things you will require before Jack is ready to be introduced to game – dummies, blank cartridge pistols, the lot.

Chapter 4

Nursery School

Once Jack has been safely vaccinated, there is one further health matter to attend to, namely to worm him at twelve or thirteen weeks. The chances are that he probably does not need it if he has been wormed twice already, but 'better safe than sorry'.

There is an old saying, 'You're never too old to learn'. Conversely, when referring to a puppy, they're never too young to learn. But nothing that would inhibit a puppy's natural inquisitiveness, development of character or general exuberance should be enforced at this early age, and certainly he should in no way be suppressed. Liken it to teaching a child the ABC, how to count, table manners and the other basics of a rational and enlightened upbringing.

As with everything else in this book, there will be people who will not agree. For example that great American trainer Charles Morgan, back in the fifties and sixties, would let his puppies 'run with the pack', hunt through the woods and let the unusual become the usual until they were twelve months or over. Above all else what he wanted them to do was to learn to hunt, flush birds and, horror of horrors, even chase rabbits! He said that you can never make a dog go if he does not have the natural inclination to do so, but you can always stop him – even if one has to revert to 'a dose of bird shot up the ass'! You can rest assured that I do not recommend this training method; it is mentioned purely to illustrate that there is more than one school of thought!

The one that I hope to demonstrate throughout this book is a progressive method whereby one does not add unnecessary work to the many hours of careful tutelage necessary to produce a top-class retriever. Charles Morgan also says that where you have just one dog, then you must become his 'buddy', the 'good guy' who will reassure him that all is well when he meets something new and, to him, spooky . You have no 'pack' for him to run with, so you have to fulfil this role. It is interesting that back in the fifties this great American trainer wrote that the friendlier you can become with your pupil, the easier it will be for you to teach, and him to absorb, 'the mechanical things that we have to do today to win a field trial'. I fully subscribe to the 'friendlier' aspect; it is an important factor. But I say definitely '*no, no no*' to any mechanical things, which, in the sense in which Morgan used it, goes completely against the whole objective of this book, namely to produce a shooting man's dog which does its job with the minimum of help and has an insatiable desire to deliver to hand.

In the very early days this can be anything from a piece of stick to a very dead and smelly rat. If it is the latter, accept it with pleasure, even if taking it turns your stomach. As far as Jack is concerned, it is, to use Charles Morgan's phraseology, an extra special gift for his 'buddy'. It must be emphasised that such gifts are only acceptable in the very early days. Once it is fully established in Jack's mind that what he finds must be brought to you, then become selective in what you will receive, and should he go to pick up 'filth' reprimand him sharply. However, this is a matter to be dealt with in a later chapter.

To return to our kindergarten training, at this stage it is necessary to state the obvious. Contrary to what some people like to believe, no dog understands every word you say. They come to relate a word or a combination of words, and most importantly the way they are intoned, to their owner's wishes. So a minimal vocabulary should be used when training. Decide what command you intend to use for a certain function and *stick to it.* The same goes for your whistle; for all normal purposes a long blast means 'stop' or 'sit', whilst short quickly repeated notes ('pip-pip-pip') mean 'come back'. Hand signals must also always be consistent. As that great trainer, the late Dick Male, was frequently heard to say, 'There's not much to training a good retriever – just repetition.' This is something of an understatement, but in essence it is the cornerstone of successful training.

There are two golden rules which the would-be trainer should get firmly instilled in his or her mind. First, never be in a hurry; each step along the road should be patiently taught so that it becomes second nature. Secondly, *never* take your dog out to train it if you have had a row or some road hog has 'cut you up' on the way home after a hard day at the office. If you do, the chances are that some small transgression on the part of your pupil may cause your pent-up anger to spill over and not only damage the bond you have worked hard to establish, but also undermine the self-assurance that he has been gaining from every lesson.

Assuming that you are using Jack's name constantly and he is hopefully beginning to respond to it, as well as becoming an enthusiastic motorist, then it is time to move on to the first lesson, one that he will undoubtedly take exception to for a short while – the introduction to a lead. The way to start is to put a small collar on him, just for a short while to begin with. Be with him and take his mind off this new and unpleasant experience; he will quickly become used to it. In a very short while he will be playing around in the garden or his kennel, oblivious to the fact that it is there. Once this stage has been reached you can dispense with the collar and put a light slip lead on him. He will no longer object to having something around his neck, but he will when restraint is placed on his movement. So for the first few lessons let him lead you. He will quickly accept the restriction of a lead and then, with very little coaxing, you will be leading him. The 'treat 'em rough school' will say it is a waste of time. Put a lead on him, they say,

Direct with hand signals for food up to 9/10 months, so that following these becomes automatic.

and if he doesn't want to come yank him along with you. He'll soon stop fighting. This is true, but why frighten the puppy and so make a backward move in the bonding process? If you have not got Jack trotting along happily on his lead in about ten days, either he is a contrary little so-and-so, or you have done something wrong.

Once he is scampering along beside you on his lead it is time for the next lesson, but remember, he is still only an 'infant', so each lesson should not extend beyond five to ten minutes and should always finish on a good note. If you have achieved your objective in a matter of a few minutes, then stop – do not keep going until your pupil starts to get bored. Once Jack is leading well, begin to teach him to walk at heel. The easiest way to do this is to swing the end of the lead, or a light garden bamboo cane, just in front of his nose. He will quickly learn to remain by your side. The occasional titbit can work wonders in maintaining interest and the correct position. Continue this lesson until he is walking freely on a completely *loose* lead by your side. Ideally his head should be just in front of your leg, so that he can mark any bird that falls on the opposite side to that on which he is heeling. When you have reached this stage it is time to see how good a teacher you have been and how good a pupil Jack is, for he needs to begin to walk at heel off the lead. Try to find a fence or hedge, where he cannot duck out to the side. To begin with either wind the lead around his neck or take it off, just laying the end across his shoulders. The bamboo can still be useful, for a gentle tap on the nose can remind your pupil that he is getting too far ahead. This is a time, too, when the odd titbit held in your left hand can be a very useful adjunct in maintaining both position and interest. To reach this stage will take a number of weeks; it is not something to rush. Heeling should become an instinct, but Jack will be long out of kindergarten by the time this stage has been reached. An important point is to vary the speed at which you walk so that, fast or slow, he is always in position. Doing U-turns and lefts and rights should all be part of the advanced part of this section of training.

It is advisable from a very early age, once Jack knows his name, to give a 'pip-pip-pip' on the whistle when calling him at all times, even if only calling him in from the garden. He will learn very quickly to respond to this and there will no longer be any need to use his name. But once he knows the call – and you are certain he knows – if he does not respond, get out after him and slip the lead on him. Then, blowing the recall on the whistle ('pip-pip-pip') yank him back to where you were originally calling him from – not too roughly, but enough to let him realise you are not pleased. Once he knows what that whistle means and does not respond he is figuratively raising two fingers vertically at you – an attitude which must be discouraged if you are to develop that rapport so essential between a Gun and his trusted and respected retriever.

Another lesson that can be learned at this stage is the command 'sit'. This can be done from a very early age and is a progressive exercise. Put your hand under his chin and, at the same time, press down gently on his hindquarters until he is sitting. To begin with do not hold him in this position for more than two or three seconds. Once he gets the idea, just put your hand under his chin, lightly pushing him back into position as you say 'Sit' and at the same time raising your other hand. You will be surprised how quickly a puppy will learn, particularly if you do it just before feeding. When he is sitting happily, full of anticipation for dinner, and you can move a step or two away from him, put his dish down and give a hand signal to direct him to it. Again there will be those who pooh-pooh this as a time-waster, but it is not, for with very little trouble you are teaching him the rudiments of hand signals, so that by the time serious training begins, following the direction in which you move your hand is a built-in reaction. This can be developed until you are able to put the bowl on either side or behind him, with the appropriate command – 'go back' in the latter case.

One final 'game' you can introduce when Jack is still in 'kindergarten' and you have reached the stage when he will sit until told to go for his food is to virtually straddle him and cup your hands together in front of him so that, when told to go, he jumps through the 'hoop' you have made. Again there will be those who will probably laugh at this, but it is all part of developing what should become an automatic reaction, to jump something when told to – it is all part of learning his ABC.

From the age of about four months start to play with Jack with a dummy. This can be a knotted handkerchief, a piece of carpet-underlay rolled up and stitched or something similar, but it should be something he likes. Further, it must be of a size that he can easily pick up. Right from the start check him; do not let him go until you send him with the command, 'Jack, hi-lost', or whatever you decided to use. If you count to two or three to begin with, this will be quite long enough to hold him at the start. The time of restraint can be increased as he gets more into the game. You should only toss the dummy a short distance to begin with, for at this age his powers of concentration are minimal. When he has reached the stage where he will sit and you can walk a few yards away from him, let him see you put the dummy somewhere where he has to stand on his hind legs to retrieve it. Later this can prove to have a twofold value. First, it will make him learn that not everything he can wind is necessarily on the ground. Secondly, if he becomes really proficient at this, then when you are shooting and walking up a heavy root crop or some other cover too tall for him to see over, he may well stand on his hind legs to see what is going on when a shot is fired. This will often enable him to mark the area in which a bird has fallen.

At around four to four and a half months, start taking Jack for very short walks on a lead, always nicely at heel. If it is wet, walk him through all the puddles you can, which will help when the time comes for him to enter water properly.

A word of warning – however brilliant your pupil may appear to be, take things slowly. There are many dogs who are spoilt, in some cases ruined beyond redemption, by trying to do too much too soon. In particular, at this early age there should be no long enforced walks. When he is over six months slowly increase the distance until, when he is around a year old they are about a mile. One not infrequently hears of puppies of four to five months being taken on 2–3-mile hikes. This is crazy! Bearing in mind that one year in a dog's life is roughly equal to seven in a human's, who in their right mind would take a two-and-a-half- to three-year-old toddler for such a walk? At the start of this book I made it clear that hip dysplasia is seldom a problem for the majority of gundogs, but extreme exercise in the case of a puppy could lead to severe damage. The cells that form when bone grows are soft, and to put it in the simplest terms, they can therefore easily be damaged by too much use before they are fully developed.

Chapter 5

Life Begins to Become Serious

Up to six or seven months, life has been a 'bowl of cherries' for young Jack, but from now on, up to fifteen to eighteen months, he really starts serious schooling. Yes, he has been learning, or he should have been if you have been following the recommendations above for his 'nursery school' days. But this period, whilst being a time for establishing the rudimentary basis for his future training, should mainly have been about developing a relationship with him, so that he has complete confidence in you.

The months leading up to this stage should also have revealed whether Jack is likely to be worth the many hours of work that are required to produce a good shooting dog. An experienced trainer would by now have assessed his worth, but this book is not written for professionals – or indeed semi-professionals – but for Guns who want an honest-to-God working gundog to find and deliver what they shoot.

So what should Jack's general demeanour be? First, he should be delighted to see you every time you are reunited having been parted. When taken out, whilst full of 'get up and go', he should by now walk to heel on command, sit whilst a dummy is tossed for him and not go until told. If he does, get out after him, grab hold of him, slip a lead on and yank him back to where he should have remained sitting. Do not be too harsh when doing this – just sufficient to let him know he has been a very bad boy. Alternatively, if you are young and strong, grab him on either side of the neck just behind the ears, lift him up and carry him back to where he was supposed to be and plonk him down, at the same time reprimanding him as you do with a stern 'NO! SIT!' You may not like doing this, for whilst you will have undoubtedly become Jack's 'buddy', it is highly likely that a reverse relationship will be developing. But obedience has to be firmly instilled into his mind, so that when at 'work' he only does what he is told, not what he thinks he would like to do. In the most

Look what I've got for you!

unlikely event that he has no interest in picking up a dummy and retrieving – and it can very occasionally happen, even with those 'bred in the purple' from a working point of view – then a nice pet home is the place for him and you should start again. However do not be put off by this comment; it is seldom a problem, but if the natural instinct and desire to do his job is missing, then he is not for you.

The choice of training ground is very important. For the next few months it is a question largely of repetition, like learning to play a musical instrument – keep practising until perfect, or as perfect as the ability of the pupil will allow. If possible choose a field or paddock with a really thick hedge, which at this stage will be like a brick wall for young Jack, and make your 'schoolroom' a corner of this field.

The time has now come for Jack to learn that, if you are going to have enjoyable days in the shooting field together, he must first learn two very important lessons: first, *never* run-in; and secondly go out to hunt and retrieve from the area that you indicate by means of hand signals, which particularly in the early days must always be clear and precise. These two important factors can be dealt with together. Prior to starting a training session let Jack have a run to let off steam before you start work. At this stage it is largely a matter of teaching him steadiness. Once he has had a run, call him up to heel and head for your training area.

When you do this, school has begun. He should be walking demurely beside you, head slightly in front of your knee, so that in due course he can mark both left and right when anything is shot. Do not get lax over this and allow sloppy heeling – no stopping to sniff this or that and dropping behind and, most importantly, when he gets older, no stopping and cocking his leg. Bad heeling is an insidious sin and if it is not checked by the time Jack joins you in the shooting field, you will walk to your peg happily chatting to your friends, and when you get there find no Jack, because he has found something of interest 50 yards or more away.

You have reached a stage when, if you are both to have enjoyable training sessions, the bonding and understanding have to become even greater. To start the lesson tell Jack to sit, walk 5–10 yards from him, face him and blow your stop whistle. Then throw a dummy over your shoulder. You should be on bare ground, so it does not matter where it goes. Watch Jack like the proverbial hawk; if he makes any attempt to go for it, be out of your starting-block quicker than Linford Christie, cut him off, grab him and unceremoniously return him whence he came. However, if his days in 'nursery school' have been correctly managed this is unlikely to happen. If all is well, raise your hand, the signal to stay. Walk out, pick up the dummy and return to Jack. At this juncture a quick pat and 'good boy', will let your pupil know he has done what you want. Walk with him still at heel, to within a yard or two of the hedge and give the command 'sit', at the same time raising your hand. Walk out just 4–5 yards from him and again blow the stop whistle, which by this time he should know means to stay until given the command to do something else. Then throw the dummy out either to the left or right of him, it doesn't matter which, and be ready to sprint out if he attempts to go before he is told. After a short pause – say a count of four or five – give the command 'hi-lost' and at the same time signal with your arm the direction he is to go – obviously towards the dummy. When he has retrieved it, praise him, walk back to where he was sitting and go through the same procedure again, this time throwing the dummy in the opposite direction. A couple more retrieves will suffice.

When he has brought you the fourth retrieve, move on a short distance with him at heel, as he always should be during a training session. Give the command 'sit', again blowing the stop whistle, and throw the dummy a good way out, where he can see it. Raise your hand, which should by now intimate to Jack that he has to stay where he is, walk out and pick the dummy up and return to him. The object of this exercise is to make Jack realise that not every dummy thrown is for him. Continue, again telling him to sit, but without blowing the stop whistle. Then when you have gone 30–40 yards whistle him up. He has to learn that when he hears 'pip-pip-pip' on your whistle this means 'come at once'. This is a time when a titbit could be given as a reward, *but never do so when he has made a retrieve*, for that could lead to him starting to drop it, a bad fault, be it dummy or bird, before it was delivered safely to hand.

Remember all youngsters can get bored, whether they are human or animal, so do not make Jack's lessons too long, otherwise he will lose interest. As a guide, twenty minutes to half an hour is quite sufficient at this stage, including walking him at heel, even less if he has done all that has been asked of him. It is important to finish on a good note. A 'run-back' is a good finale. Let Jack see you drop a dummy, then walk on with him at heel, to begin with about 15–20 yards. Give the command to sit and blow the stop whistle, then walk on another 5–10 yards, turn, give the command 'get back' and, at the same time, give a hand signal – your arm up in the air, almost straight and in a position which can only really be described as a straight-armed throw. Jack should race back and pick the dummy. If he is coming back with it to you *do not blow your recall whistle*; he is doing what you asked. This is a very common failing, which one frequently sees at novice working tests, and indeed at novice field trials. Further, do not call him by name (unless he happens to be dawdling and needs to be encouraged to hurry up) and do not stand with your arms outstretched. Jack knows where you are – he must do if he is galloping back to you – so there is no need to try and take on the appearance of an animated scarecrow!

After a few days of these initial exercises it is time to move on. Sit Jack down as you have been doing, walk away and go through the same procedure as before, but now throw dummies to both his left and his right. Always, in these early days, send him for the *first* one thrown. His natural inclination will be to go for the last, so be on your toes, ready to stop him if necessary. However, once

Left to right. Sit on command to whistle and hand, note right arm raised; dog should automatically look to his/her left, as arm moves to handler's right dog should be ready to go in that direction on hearing his name. Arm fully extended, body leaning in the direction the dog is to go. A step in the required direction is also helpful.

he realises that he will eventually be allowed to get both, and that his 'buddy' is not too happy if he has ideas of his own, the penny will soon drop that the direction you indicate with your arm is the direction he has to go.

Having responded to the command and signal and retrieved the dummy, walk Jack back to where he was. Go through the same routine to sit and stay and toss a third dummy back to where the first one was thrown. Then go back to where you were 'handling' from before and give Jack the command to retrieve the *second* dummy. Do not let him fetch the one you have just put out. When he has retrieved dummy number two, take it from him, tell him to sit, raise your arm and at the same time blow the stop whistle. Do not forget the pattern you have decided on and adhere to it rigidly in these early days. It may sound a bit excessive to the uninitiated, but at this stage it is all about repetition. If the sequence is broken it can confuse your pupil and land you with extra work.

When you think Jack has the above firmly fixed in his mind, then it is time to take the next step. Go through the same routine as for a dummy on either side, but this time lob one onto the ground between you and him. Give a rather elongated version of the recall 'pip-pip-pip' on the whistle and at the same time raise your arm slightly above shoulder height and bring it down towards the ground – a signal to come towards you. It is absolutely essential to be clear with these signals. Working only yards away it may sound relatively unimportant, but later in life, when you are shooting and you have seen a bird fall that Jack has been unable to mark, then it matters. If you have established a good rapport, it is essential that he knows, via the medium of hand signals, where you want him to hunt. This does not mean that he must be guided right to wherever it is he is to retrieve – far from it. But it is a great help to be able to direct him into the area where he is to hunt. It is equally desirable to establish that particular note on your whistle, akin to the recall *but not the same*, to draw him in towards you when he is out hunting.

When Jack is picking dummies to his left, to his right and in towards you, then it is time to cover the final point – straight behind him. Part of the work for this will already have been done by the 'fun' run-backs at the end of a training session. Drop a dummy so that he sees it, walk on about 15 yards, sit him as for the other dummy positions, walk on a similar distance, turn and give the command 'go back' and the 'go back' signal already referred to. When you feel confident that he fully understands both commands and signals, then sit him and put out four dummies – left, right, in front and behind – and send him for the one you want. The first time you do this be on your toes and make sure he retrieves according to your commands. Once you are satisfied he knows left from right, backwards or inwards then you can move on. It is advisable, however, to go through this exercise once or twice a week for a while, even when he is further advanced in his training.

There are just a few little pointers to work in with the above. Hopefully Jack will come tearing back like the proverbial 'bat out of hell' with the dummy, but you may be anticipating a nice clean retrieve right into your hands, when he suddenly swerves around you. Of course this could be due to a number of things – for example, 'I found it, it's mine and I'm going to keep it.' Or maybe it is just a mixture of devilment and high spirits. But there could be another reason. Compare your size with Jack's. You are many times his size and consequently, when he is still very young and as yet untutored, seeing you standing there, normally with your legs pretty close together, your legs may suddenly take on the appearance of a brick wall. If you have any brains you do not rush headlong into a brick wall; if possible you stop or try to

Once pupil understands signals, both from whistle and hand, when at a distance it is not necessary for Jack to sit. He should stop, facing handler and await directions.

swerve around it. That is what sometimes happens with a puppy, who may thus develop the infuriating habit of not bringing a retrieve straight to hand. So, during the early days of retrieving, when waiting to take a dummy from Jack, stand with your legs wide apart – there is then light in the 'wall', a way through, so there is no need for him to take evasive action. Of course, there is no certainty that he would have ducked round you if you had your legs together, but it is much easier to avoid a problem than to cure one. Of course there will be those who scoff at such a precaution, but when a point has been successfully proved on a number of occasions, why knock it?

Here is another word of warning. Whilst you are aiming at a quick, clean delivery into your hands, whatever you do do not encourage Jack to jump up with his offering, be it a dummy, or a duck from the muddy edge of a lake. Some years ago, one of the country's leading professional trainers started teaching his pupils to do this. He had a very promising youngster, with which he expected to do great things. All was going well until he was running in a field trial under one of the most senior Kennel Club judges. The dog made a spectacular retrieve from wet and muddy conditions, and came back at full speed, finishing up delivering the bird with his paws on the handler's chest. The owner was instructed to put his dog on the lead, as he was no longer wanted.

He was told that a Gun did not want a wet and muddy dog jumping all over him every time he made a retrieve on a day's shooting – certainly a very valid point.

A few words on the subject of dummies. As I have said, dummies are obtainable from Turner Richards, but a variety of dummies will make Jack's life more interesting. They are easy to make. Cut a piece of wood about 1 in × 1½ in and 10 in long, nail a length of cord, some 6–7 in, to it. Then roll carpet underlay around it until it is about 3–4 in in diameter, or even a little more, and cover it with a piece of strong sacking or a sock. Make certain that whatever you use as covering is firmly held in place by a strong adhesive. It is quite a good idea to make dummies of different diameters as, in the early stages of training, a slimmer one will be easier for a puppy to balance and carry.

To help Jack to learn about balance, a useful tip is to take something like a washing-up liquid bottle and fill it about one-third with sand, covering it with a sock and making sure there are no loose bits by which he can pick it up. He will quickly learn that if he picks it up centrally it will be much easier to carry than lifting it at the end. Weight is another factor to consider when making up training dummies. The average throwing dummy one can purchase weighs 1 lb, but one can buy them weighing up to 3 lb. When it comes to the real thing, a good partridge weighs 1 lb or an ounce or two over, pheasants can vary from 2–3½ lb, a mallard, in good condition, 3–3½ lb and a hare 6–8 lb, or in some cases more. It is, therefore, a good idea to make up a heavy dummy or two. The simplest way to obtain weight is by filling a large washing-up liquid bottle, or something similar, with sand and then encasing it in carpet underlay or a sock. Alternatively, it is possible to buy a hare dummy from Turner Richards, weighted at both ends with a pliable mid-section which hopefully teaches the pupil to lift and correctly balance its retrieve. However, weight need not enter the equation at this stage; it is something to be considered at a later date. There are in fact a great range of dummies that can be bought, some realistically painted to represent feathered quarry. These may well give pleasure to the purchaser, but such artistic embellishments are no help to Jack, for he only sees in shades of grey.

Chapter 6

Introduction to Gunfire

By now Jack should have become fairly adept at taking hand signals, and you should be able to send him left, right, back or draw him towards you. He should also, of course, be walking tight to heel, sitting whilst you toss dummies around and go and pick them up yourself, and doing run-backs. It is now time to take the next step, a most crucial one: the introduction to gunfire.

This can be started quite early in a puppy's life, first by banging feeding tins together just before dishing out the food. Jack will quickly learn to look upon this noise as the dinner gong rather than a disturbing noise. A child's cap pistol is also a useful adjunct, fired first at the same time as banging feeding bowls together, then on its own. If you get no adverse reaction to this at four to five months, it is unlikely that you will meet any problems.

One day, when all has gone well at your training area, sit Jack down, walk away about 20 yards and fire a blank cartridge pistol. If you have accustomed him to lesser bangs he should take no notice. If this is the case, return to him, give him a pat and tell him what a good boy he is. If you get an adverse reaction, however, and he tries to slink off, do not rush after him, drag him back to where he was, hold him and start firing over him. Oh yes, such stupidity has been known, and it will quickly ruin a dog for life. In the unlikely event that he takes exception to the pistol and shows a certain amount of concern, do not push your luck – there is always tomorrow. Training a Retriever to become a good gundog takes time, patience and understanding. If he is worried try and get someone to join you when training and fire some blanks 80–100 yards away to start with, whilst you stand with Jack to give him confidence as he looks, listens and learns. If he is just mildly gun nervous this can quickly be overcome. It often helps if you or a friend have an experienced dog to come and sit with Jack. He will quickly cotton on to the fact that his companion is not in the least concerned and in no time at all he will be the same.

Having overcome any possible preliminary nerves, gradually move close with your blank cartridge pistol until you can stand beside him and fire it. Once you are completely happy that bangs do not worry him, take a dummy with you and throw it up in the air to land as close as possible to you, firing a shot as you do so. Do not let Jack pick it up; collect it yourself. At this stage all you are aiming for is to develop a train of thought – that a shot equals a possible retrieve. Whilst you are doing this, however, you are at the same time strengthening the earlier lesson that Jack must not move until told.

Having established that he is not in the least gun shy, the next thing on the curriculum is to walk him, at heel, with a gun under your arm. Start to swing it about as though shooting at imaginary targets, until he pays no attention to it. If you are right-handed, Jack will be at heel on your left, whilst you carry your gun under your right arm. If, however, you are left-handed then Jack should be taught to heel on your right; for if he is heeling on the same side as you carry your gun, then you could give him a crack over the head with the end of the barrel. There is also the million-to-one chance of a Gun breaking all the rules of safety and walking along with a loaded and cocked gun tucked under his arm and the trigger catching on something. I know of two such incidents where the gun has gone off and killed the dogs. Of course, it never would have happened if the most basic safety rules had been followed, but they were not and accidents happen through such lapses. So why take such a risk?

Having got Jack used to a blank cartridge pistol being fired, to the extent that he pays no attention, other than possible signs of expectation that something is about to happen, graduate to a .410. Sit Jack down 3–4 yards from you, rest the loaded gun on your shoulder pointing upwards at an angle of about 80 degrees, then throw a dummy up, as you did when using blanks, to land as close as possible to you, at the same time fire the gun. It is most unlikely that you will get any adverse reaction. When you are confident that Jack is not the least concerned, do the same thing with the type of shotgun you use. Normally this should only take a few days. There is a reason for not firing your gun straight over your and Jack's heads, particularly when you get to a bigger bore than a .410, for what goes up must come down and you do not want shot raining down on him. Of course it would not hurt him, but it might just worry him slightly and that is something to avoid throughout training, except when you tell him he has been a naughty boy.

People can quite unintentionally do very, very silly things when training, particularly if they are trying to speed up the process. A good example that comes to mind relates to a very keen shot who was always in a hurry over everything he did. He had bought and worked several trained dogs over the years, then he decided to train a very promising twelve-month-old Labrador himself. The pup was doing remarkably well considering the intensive course he was being put through. However, it was getting very close to the start of the shooting season; it was only weeks away and the dog was not 100 per cent happy with the gun, simply because the introduction had been wrong. So the owner arranged for one of his gamekeepers to put twenty clays over him from the top of a high bank as fast as possible. His totally erroneous theory was that when the barrage was over it would have allayed any worries the dog might have regarding gunfire. As you can imagine, the dog, which had been tethered, was terrified, and from then on was useless. There really are no short cuts if you want to finish up with a well-behaved, biddable dog.

The next stage is to walk around in a field, along a hedgerow or through a wood, it does not really matter, with Jack at heel. Suddenly throw up the gun and fire it, perhaps at imaginary cock high over the trees, or a rabbit scurrying into its burrow in the hedge. Once he is totally unconcerned by this, walk with him at heel, drop a dummy that he can see, continue on – and here it helps if you have a friend to do this – then throw a dummy out in front of you while you fire a shot in its general direction. Then send Jack back for the one you dropped. When he has retrieved it to hand, tell him to sit, not forgetting to go through the routine of using the stop whistle and raised hand, before he picks up the 'shot' dummy. The chief objective of this exercise is to teach him first that he does not run in to shot, and secondly that he goes where you say, not where he would like to go – the 'shot' dummy is obviously the more exciting. This exercise goes one step further when you drop a dummy that he does not see, making the temptation to retrieve the dummy out in front all the greater. Once it is clear that Jack knows he only retrieves what you send him for, start to alternate by sending either for the 'blind' or the 'shot' dummy first.

Whilst teaching these new lesson, keep making Jack go through what he has already learned when you are out working him. By doing this the basic alphabet of training becomes second nature. Never go on so long that he becomes fed up and uninterested, and always try and finish each session on a high note.

Chapter 7

Developing Memory and Straight Running

You have been developing Jack's memory since his kindergarten days, but this has been what might be described as 'instant memory'. He will now have reached the stage when the time factor increases gradually from seconds to minutes. We have touched on the question of short run-backs; now both time and distance become longer.

To begin with tell him to sit and toss a dummy back in the direction from which you have just come, preferably into the wind so that when he is sent back for it it is in his favour. Then, telling Jack to heel, walk away from the dummy. Watch him; normally you can tell if a dog is losing interest in what you have dropped – his memory starts waning. As soon as you think this is happening, turn, tell him to sit and then give the command 'go back'. If may sound unnecessary, but, during these formative days, you should always give the correct body and arm signal in conjunction with the verbal command. Some people blow the stop whistle as their dog goes back for a dummy, but I do not recommend it, at least in the early stages. Yes, he should by now stop immediately, but you will break his concentration and as you have been blowing it at him since he was a pup, what is the point? You can do this later perhaps, but not at this stage; the object of the run-back is *memory development*. If you stop him for no good reason, he will start to pre-empt your instruction, suddenly halt, look round and wait for you to signal and again give the command 'go back'. This can become very tedious and is what in the USA is referred to as 'popping'. One sees it, thankfully only occasionally, in dogs that have started life as test dogs and then graduated to the real thing. They are in fact relying too much on their handler and not on their own ability to find game or dummies – a trait you certainly do not want to develop in Jack.

Opposite and right: Utilizing modern farming and tramlines, putting out three consecutive dummies to develop memory and straight running.

To begin with, do not try to be clever and throw the dummy into a difficult place. You are not trying to outwit him, your aim is to develop his ability to remember where something has fallen and *retain that memory*. The simplest way to do this is to keep increasing the distance of the run-backs, until he can go back 150–200 yards spot on to where you dropped the dummy. When this has become second nature, let Jack see you throw a dummy a short way into cover, but initially over shorter distances. If you have been giving him run-backs along a ride in a wood, that simplifies matters. Go through what has now become yet another routine exercise, but instead of dropping the dummy where Jack can see it on the ride, toss it into the cover at the side – nothing too testing at this stage, the chief objective is to ensure that he remembers where to turn off into the wood. This is normally no problem and it becomes a matter of progression – increasing the distance and making the retrieves more difficult from heavier cover. One other useful addition to this part of his training is to put a dummy up in a bush, brambles, or even the low fork of a

Lining up to send.

Dog going for a
retrieve, having
received the
appropriate
command.

First dummy
retrieved to hand
– two more to
remember.

tree, but always be careful that it is so placed that it does not get
wedged. Not all shot game make it to the ground and it is as well
that Jack should be made aware of this.

When a run-back has become an almost reflex activity, you
can capitalize on this to help increase his steadiness by creating
diversions, for example throwing a dummy towards, but to the
side of him, as he comes galloping back. Another ploy is to have
someone send a Retriever Ball (obtainable from Turner
Richards) racing across the ground just in front of him as he is
returning. An alternative ruse is to use a dummy covered with a
rabbit skin, attached to a length of strong elastic, about ⅜ in
square, firmly pegged to the ground, then stretched taut across
Jack's line of return. Ask someone to hold the dummy and, as Jack
approaches the 'rabbit run', release it so that it whips across in
front of him. If he succumbs to the temptation of any of these
diversions, get out after him fast and impress upon him that he
does not chase anything for which he has not been sent. Unless
you are training dogs all the time it really is not worth rigging up
an 'elastic rabbit', for few dogs ever fall into that trap a second
time – a forcibly bowled Retriever Ball is equally good and can
have other uses.

These exercises will improve Jack's memory and ensure that he will go out in a straight line for a run-back or to a mark, but what about running straight without having seen anything down? In the past some trainers would cut a narrow swath through tallish grass, sit the dog at the end if it, walk out and drop a dummy when facing the dog, and shout 'mark'. They would then go back to the pupil and, lining up both body and hand signal, send for it – really elementary stuff. Having done this a few times, they would drop the first dummy as 'seen', continue another 10 yards or so and drop a second but unseen one. The first one of course was easy. On receiving this they would line the dog up again and, hopefully, it would go out again along where the path had been cut. Should it deviate from the straight and narrow, it would be quickly brought back into line and, if necessary, taken up to within a yard or two of the second dummy. Like so much of a dog's training it then became a matter of repetition. When two dummies were being picked without any problem, then a third, again unseen, would be added. Once all three were being retrieved, then still keeping the same line a dummy would be placed, again unseen, in the long grass beyond the end of the swath. To begin with this would be just a matter of a few yards and probably only one dummy put out towards the end of the lane. Once the pupil was going straight up the cut area and continuing on, then the training run was dispensed with and the lesson merged into a general training session.

If you live in an area where there are no arable crops, then undoubtedly cutting a swath through grass is a great asset in developing straight running. However, if you live, as I do, where there is a large acreage of corn and sugar beet grown, then modern farming saves you the trouble, unless it happens to be an organically grown crop. Both corn and beet fields are regularly fertilized or sprayed, the tractors following the same 'tram lines' which provide ideal 'runs' to train Jack, as is illustrated by the foregoing photographs. These 'tram lines' have a great advantage over a path cut through grass, as many, at least in this area, are hundreds of yards in length. This will enable you to put out a marker(s) at varying distances, opposite which you can place a retrieve in cover. You can then send Jack in a straight line until he reaches a marker, stop him on the whistle and signal him in the direction in which you wish him to hunt for a 'blind', be it a dummy or cold game that you have previously put out.

Chapter 8

Introduction to Fur and Feather

Now it is time to move on to what all the hours of patient dummy training have been leading up to – the start of Jack eventually 'earning his keep' and, probably, a place in your heart, by beginning to show that he can really be 'a dog for your game'. To quote from the Preface to a book by that great author Patrick Chalmers, whose work back in the twenties and thirties enthralled so many people, '"What fun," a youthful Guardsman is reported to have exclaimed, as he "larked" home to Melton after a blank day, "what fun fox-hunting would be *if it wasn't for those damned hounds*!" Plagiarising this Nimroditty, most of us who are not super-shots, will say, "What *poor* fun would shooting be without shooting-dogs. For what makes more for the enjoyment of a day's shooting than a good gun-dog?"' Yes indeed! For many, a day out with the gun, unaccompanied by a shooting companion, be it Labrador, Golden Retriever, Flatcoat or Spaniel, would be something akin to a gin and tonic without the gin – for a major ingredient for full enjoyment would be missing.

When you are reasonably satisfied with Jack's work on dummies, which will probably be by the time he is nine to twelve months old, then he should be introduced to 'fur' and 'feather'. It is a good idea to have pickled a few pheasant and wild duck wings from the previous season in readiness for this. The pickling is a simple process – a mixture of salt and alum rubbed into where the wing has been severed from the body and then the 'meaty' bit left in this mixture for a few days. Once dry such wings will last for a considerable time.

It is possible to purchase white feather and canvas wraps to fit around a dummy, but I do not recommend these. The reason is that although dogs only see in shades of grey, white becomes a very pale grey against a background of green grass or plough, which can result in a youngster looking for his retrieves rather than seeking them through the use of his nose.

The main objective of this part of the training is to get Jack used to the feel of feather in his mouth. Wings can easily be attached to a dummy with the aid of a couple of good stout elastic bands. Make sure they are securely attached, for, when you throw the dummy, you do not want it going one way and the wings another – this would be somewhat confusing for Jack, to say the least. This has happened more than once. Should this occur to you when you have Jack out training, leave him sitting and go and pick up the bits and start again. But before throwing your feathered dummy, show it to Jack, let him sniff it and hold it, for it is very different from the canvas and sock dummies to which he has become accustomed.

When Jack goes for a walk with you, he cannot be permanently at heel, for like all children he must be allowed to have a good romp around, explore, and, as Charles Morgan says, 'let the unusual become the usual'. But there is a very strong likelihood that he will find some carrion and think, 'Ah, this is just what the boss would like.' Whatever it is, at this stage, let him know how delighted you are at receiving such a gift – in the not too distant future he will learn how contrary humans can become, for he will get thoroughly told off for picking up such dirt. However, as yet he is not sufficiently advanced to be taught what is an acceptable 'gift' and what is not.

Should he prove to be difficult about picking 'feather', just try one feather attached to either side of a dummy, or, alternatively, make him sit, put a wing in his mouth and make him hold it. If he does so without too much fuss, put a hand under his jaw and walk backwards, with him carrying the wing. If this seems to be going all right, put a pair of wings on a dummy with a small circumference and do the same thing. If he holds it, then the chances are your problem is solved. It should, however, be stressed that normally there is little or no bother over this – just occasionally. One case comes to mind where a trainer was getting desperate with a puppy who had shown great promise until he was asked to pick a winged dummy. He would not even sit and hold a wing. The trainer had nearly given up when one day he was giving the pup a run with some older dogs, when it found a very dead blackbird and came racing back, delivering it nicely to hand. The handler immediately returned to the kennels, took the wings off the remains of the blackbird and attached them to a puppy dummy. He threw it for the youngster and it was retrieved without any problem. The trainer then added two pheasant wings, putting the blackbird's on top of them. Again there was a nice quick retrieve. Next day, after one retrieve of the blackbird/pheasant dummy, the trainer removed the blackbird wings, rubbed the rotting remains of the blackbird over another new set of wings and tried again. This also resulted in a quick, pleasing retrieve, and from then on the pup never looked back.

When Jack is retrieving winged dummies with no problem, attach a bird wing with a short piece of string or twine to the end where the throwing toggle or cord is attached. When you throw it, the loose wing will spin around, giving the appearance, if you have a vivid imagination, of a falling pheasant. You will find it will arouse Jack's interest even further.

Whilst obtaining 'feather' occasionally causes a problem (although game can be bought for a modest sum from most shoots) this is seldom a problem with 'fur'. In the country there should be little or no problem in obtaining a few rabbit skins. To make life easier (and less smelly as time goes by) tack the skins out on a piece of board, having scraped off any fat, and rub a little salt and alum into them. When dry the skins should be reasonably pliable and can easily be wrapped around a dummy. Having got Jack picking both 'fur' and 'feather' with the same enthusiasm as he has been plain dummies, it is time for the next step – cold game.

In days gone by, it was customary for the gentry to foregather for a slap-up meal after a good day's hunting or shooting, and when the ladies had left the dining room, there was a customary toast: 'The ladies, God bless 'em.' God bless 'em indeed, for without the ladies there would be no stockings or tights, and they play an integral part in Jack's introduction to cold game. It is advisable, to begin with, to put whatever kind of bird you use in a nylon stocking. A whole bird smells, feels and tastes different from the winged dummies you have been working, so it is advisable to make the change as gradual as possible. They feel very different to our hands, so imagine how much more different they will feel to Jack when he first takes them into his mouth. Once again, should this stage of training be reached out of the shooting season, a little foresight during the previous one will be a help: put a few partridges and hen pheasants in your freezer. Pigeons are all right to use in a nylon stocking, if nothing else is available, but I recommend that they are used only once. Indeed, this applies to all birds in the early days of training on cold game.

Once Jack is bringing back the nylon-clad birds quickly and

delivering cleanly to hand, you can dispense with the covering and let him have a feel of the real thing. Let him hold it first and be prepared to slip your finger in over his lower lip, pressing down hard on to the teeth if he grabs at it, giving the command 'gently, gently'. Again, if your training to date has gone as planned, you should have no trouble. Whatever game you use, make sure it is a case of one bird, one retrieve, preferably a clean one with no blood, even dry. Teal are ideal because they are small, but any wild duck are equally suitable, because the feathers do not come out. If you use a bird more than once, certainly in the early days, it will only lead to 'mouthing' once the feathers become wet from saliva and that, in turn, can lead to a hard mouth. Remember that Jack will find dead birds, whatever they are, very much more exciting than dummies, so one or two retrieves on cold game at the end of a training session on dummies is all that is required. Up to this stage all retrieves have been off bare or nearly bare ground. However, ideally, from now on very light cover should be used, in the form of grass just tall enough so that the bird is not visible. There are two reasons for this. Cold game is exciting and if Jack becomes what is described as a hard-going dog – one with plenty of drive and verve – a bird that lies out in the open, easily seen from where you send him, might cause him to grab it up with so much enthusiasm that he damages it. A little bit of cover just slows him down sufficiently, at the same time making him realise that he has a nose and hopefully ensuring that he picks his bird just that little bit more slowly and thus more tenderly, than he might have done if grabbing it up at full gallop. Again such a precaution need only apply until 'the unusual becomes the usual'.

Earlier I suggested that, to begin with, only hen pheasants and partridges are used. The reason is that Jack has been working on dummies that weigh around 1 lb, while a cock pheasant can weigh up to 3½ lb. So something lighter will be fairer and, most importantly, easier for him to pick up cleanly. Dummies are reasonably symmetrical and Jack has learned how to balance and handle these. But until he learns how to gather it up, a big old cock pheasant is a totally different kettle of fish. Woodpigeons can be used, but they are not very desirable because the feathers come out very easily and Jack would not be too thrilled by a mouthful of these. If it becomes truly necessary, then I suggest that you tuck the head under the wing and put a strong rubber band around it. This will help lessen the chances of Jack getting a mouth full of feathers. Feral pigeons, which are basically racing homers, and are seen in many towns and cities throughout the country, often in the vicinity of grain stores, are fine, for their feathers do not come out like those of a woodpigeon. It is probable that, in the years to come, Jack will be asked to pick other game in addition to those named – specifically snipe and woodcock. These both obviously have an entirely different taste from normal game, and dogs which are not trained to them find them distasteful and will not pick them up. So early in life, he should be introduced to starlings, or possibly rooks, which are equally unpleasant from Jack's point of view. If he picks these he will certainly retrieve both snipe and woodcock. Should you have problems with this then it means having to get hold of another pair of tights and go through the whole procedure again. But it will be worth it in the end, for if you have patience and understanding, combined with equal portions of discipline and praise, you will be well on the way to achieving your objective.

Chapter 9

Retrieving Over Jumps

The first point to make about jumping – and a very important one – is not to start it until Jack has stopped growing bone, which will be when he is around ten to twelve months. He will mature and take on the appearance of an adult, but not until after his actual skeletal structure is complete, and it is the latter that is important. Bone grows, to put it at its simplest, by the development of more cells. When first formed these are soft and, just as excessive walking with a puppy can lead to hip dysplasia, so excessive early jumping can be the cause of damage – not often, but why take risks?

In Chapter 4 I suggested that you straddle Jack once he has learned to sit, lean over him and cup your hands to make a hoop for him to pop through to get his dinner. There is nothing very spectacular about this, but it develops the idea in his mind that he can get all four feet off the ground at the same time. Then, when he is five or six months old, you can encourage him, when out on a short walk, to follow you over a small fallen tree trunk which you can step over with ease but is big enough to become an obstacle requiring him to jump, even if only inches off the ground. Maybe there is somewhere you can go where there is a small ditch, which you can take in your stride, but requires Jack to take a small leap to get across. When he is doing this, toss a puppy dummy over for him to retrieve, giving the command 'hi-over' – nothing big, nothing that will jar him when landing, just fun, but all part of the two key factors that should run throughout your training, namely repetition and developing each essential so that it becomes second nature.

When the time comes to start serious jumping, much depends on how much effort you are prepared to put into it. Ideally you want to construct a jumping lane, smaller but similar to those used for horses. You can build one in your garden; if you are fortunate enough to have a good solid hedge on one side of your lawn, your

Jumping is something that can be taught in the garden.

problem is half solved. All you then want is some wire netting,
3–4 ft tall. Old-fashioned sheep netting with 4-in mesh is ideal,
and, of course, the bigger the mesh the cheaper the wire. Put this
up about 3 ft from the hedge by threading light stakes through it
– even strong bamboos will do, providing there is a reasonably
strong post at either end. It is important that the opposite end to
that from where you are sending is closed off, as you do not want
Jack to try to take any short cuts. He must come back to where
he was sent from. Training should be a forward-thinking process,
and if it is your intention to make a jumping lane eventually, then
it could easily be of use in the very early days of training, when
a puppy may think that 'finders is keepers', and try to run off with

Boldly back from cover.

a dummy; in a lane they have nowhere to go but back to their trainer.

Once the lane has been erected – and, providing it is tall enough, it can be wire on either side – then it is a case of building your jumps. Start with something solid, as this eliminates any temptation to push through. A couple of uprights on either side of the lane into which you can slot boards so as to raise the height as required, are a good idea. A length of rabbit netting, like that found around young plantations, makes a good second fence, but to begin with fix a piece of wood across the top and a few twigs, anything that clearly shows the wire is there and stops a puppy thinking that because there is light it can run through it. After a few goes over the course you can dispense with whatever you have put on the wire to indicate there is a barrier across the lane, and leave it as a straightforward jump over wire. Another useful idea is to make a small gate, through which Jack can see between

Beecher's Brook would be no obstacle!

the bars but finds they are just too close to get through and so has to jump.

It is advisable to introduce Jack to each fence separately and, when he has gained confidence over each one, send him down over them all to retrieve a dummy from the far end. From then on, when out walking or training watch out for any suitable jumps to send him over, so that once again the unusual becomes the usual.

Lady Hill-Wood used to say that she always kept two or three dummies in her car and, if she had any of her dogs with her when travelling around the country and saw what could be an unusual and testing retrieve, she would stop and give them a run, in the hope that she would never get caught out, either in a field trial or on a day's shooting, by the unexpected. Eric Baldwin had a section of plaited garden fencing fitted with feet, like a show jump for horses, 3 ft 6 in high and 6 ft wide. This he would move around in the paddock where he trained, and with open stake dogs he would send them out to it, pip them up, then give the command 'over'. Invariably they flew over the fence, there would be a dummy on the landing side and woe betide one if it did not come back over the hurdle, even if it was 100 yards away!

Do not attach a length of barbed wire to the top of your rabbit-netting fence in the mistaken belief that if Jack scratches himself a few times it will make him jump higher. Frequently contact with barbed wire can produce a far more serious injury than a scratch. Annex B to the J Regulations, J(B), Section 3f of the Kennel Club's *Guide to the Conduct of Field Trials*, reads, 'Judges should be careful for the safety of the dogs and should not require them to negotiate hazards such as dangerous barbed-wire fences, ice on ponds, unsupervised roadways, walls with high drops.' When working Jack in the future, when he has graduated to the shooting field, always remember this. A lost pheasant or partridge will probably be worth £1 to £2, but if you have done your training properly, to replace Jack would cost at least £1,500, probably more.

Chapter 10

Hunting for and Retrieving Blinds

Up to this stage all Jack's retrieves have been from bare ground, where they have been easily visible, but now the time has come for him to learn to use his nose. His olfactory senses are vastly greater than ours, but even so they have to be developed. He has, quite simply, to learn to use them and believe what they tell him.

To begin with go back to the corner of the field where you started training if the grass has grown; if it has not, find another similar spot. It is important that Jack learns to hunt within a confined space (to hold his ground) to start with, and that you do not give him the opportunity of straying out of the 'area of the fall' so that you have to keep stopping him on the whistle to bring him back to where he should be. This could lead to the development of an unacceptable trait for a gundog, namely constantly looking for guidance from his owner. It is something one sees more and more these days in dogs that have graduated into field trials via working tests.

Before going any further, a few words on scenting artificial retrieves are needed. Human scent is very strong; it does not matter how much you wash! Many wild animals can detect the presence of a man with ease if they are downwind of him. So just handling an object to be retrieved will immediately make it easier to find. This, incidentally, is why the Kennel Club say that, in a field trial, once game has been handled it cannot be used for any purpose again, except to throw one into water for a dog to gain its water certificate, which is mandatory before a dog can become a field trial champion – but in that case it is the entry into the water which is being assessed, not the actual retrieve.

The majority of training is done through the spring and summer months, and many trainers tuck the dummies under their arms when they perspire on a hot day. For those who might

FT Ch Lafayette Tolley returning with a long blind from sugar beet.

be a bit squeamish about this, it is possible to purchase little bottles of Trailmaster. It is American and can be obtained from Turner Richards. The scents are said to be natural – rabbit, pheasant or duck – but no human could tell. Suffice to say a few drops on a new dummy will give it scent.

Having found a suitable spot with *soft* cover – grass, or young corn 6–9 in tall, sit Jack down and throw two or three tennis balls out into it – about 12–18 yards is quite far enough, but be very careful that they are spaced in such a way that when he picks one and is returning, he does not run across another and change balls. Always throw them into the wind so that their scent meets him as he hunts. Obviously if you throw them downwind then the scent will blow away from him and he will have to be whistled back to where you have thrown them. Hold him for a few seconds before sending him, but remember to choose a place where he is unable to leave the area where the balls have fallen. Much then depends on how good a job he makes of it. If he really works the ground well and makes a quick find – great. Tell him to sit, wait for longer than the first time, and then send him out once more. There may be a great temptation to help him, but providing he stays where you want him to be, leave him alone to get on with his job. Only as a final resort walk out and help him. Take him up within feet of a ball if necessary, encouraging him all the while, for it is most important that he has a find. Having done this a number of times, move on to the next phase.

Again this should be in a corner of a field, where Jack cannot escape. Having told him to sit, throw out half a dozen well-scented dummies, each time giving the command 'mark'. Next comes the tricky bit. Leaving Jack, walk out and pick up five, each time trying to position yourself between Jack and the dummy so that he cannot see what you are doing. Then return to him and send him, with the usual command that you have used all along, such as 'hi-lost', at the same time indicating the direction he is to go (although he should know this, having marked the falls). He should hold his ground, acknowledging the falls as he finds them, until he picks up the sixth dummy. Whilst he is doing this, making sure he does not see you, toss a dummy out at about 45 degrees to the line he went out on. If he fails to pick the sixth dummy, stop him on the whistle and handle him onto the dummy you have just thrown. Should he pick the sixth dummy *after* you have thrown out an extra one, when retrieved, leave him sitting whilst you collect *whichever* dummy has not been picked by Jack. It is most important that he has a retrieve, for with constant failure he could easily lose interest at this age. Apart from increasing his hunting ability, it also helps develop his memory. Like his other faculties this has to be broadened and utilised as part of his education.

When you are satisfied that he has cottoned on to the idea that he has to use his nose when hunting, then it is time to make it even more interesting and to start to use cold game. The procedure is much the same to begin with: but a bit of guile is essential, so that Jack does not see what you are doing. First, throw a bird – preferably game or a duck, but not pigeon, unless it is a feral one – out *into the wind*, making sure that Jack marks it. To help you in the subterfuge that follows, attach a piece of fine string or fishing line around the neck of the retrieve, leaving a small loop, and have about 4 yards of nylon fishing line ready. Walk out to the bird you have thrown, being sure to position yourself, as far as is possible, so that Jack cannot see what you are doing. Pick up the bird, quickly slip one end of the nylon line through the loop, keeping the two loose ends in one hand, whilst holding it up out of Jack's sight with the other. Walk on, always into the wind, for 3 or 4 yards and, still screening what you are doing from your pupil, put the bird on the ground and literally rub the earth with it so as to be certain that there is scent. Lift it up in front of you with the nylon line, walk on for a further two or three strides and go through the same procedure. Then go on

8–10 yards, dropping the retrieve once again so that Jack cannot see. Release one end of the line, which will, of course, pull out through the loop as you walk on, leaving the bird on the ground. Return to Jack, skirting around the area where you have been leaving patches of scent for him to find as he hunts. By this time your pupil's memory should have developed to a degree that he will remember where he marked the fall. He should own this and begin to work the ground. If he heads straight out towards the second drop, all well and good. However, if he does not, stop him on the whistle at once and signal him in the right direction. Hopefully he will own the next 'fall', then the next, and finally pick the bird. Do not become despondent if all does not go as you hoped at the first attempt. Remember the two main factors in making a top-class gundog, after a natural inherent aptitude: loads of patience on your part, and our old friend repetition. In this exercise you are adding two things to Jack's fund of knowledge: first, handling onto a 'blind' should he need help (and the chances are he will); and, secondly the first steps towards learning how to take a runner.

When you are satisfied that the most recent lesson is safely stored away in Jack's brain, then it is time to add to his repertoire and move on to the next lesson. For this you require a helper. Get someone to throw a dummy, preferably from cover where he or she cannot be seen, into lightish cover, 25–30 yards away – a mark that Jack can clearly see. Do not be surprised if he marks short of the fall to begin with. His view is from about 2 feet above the ground; you see the fall from 3–4 feet higher than he does. If you are lissom enough to get down to Jack's viewing point you will understand why he thinks the dummy is closer than it really is. However, he will soon adjust and know to go that little bit further. Send him for it and even if you know he has marked the fall give the appropriate hand signal. It is a good idea, right from the start, to turn your whole body so that in time Jack will come to realise that both your hand signal and forward foot point in the direction he has to go. As he gallops back with the dummy, have your helper throw another into the same place. Having received the first one, line Jack up and give whatever command you have chosen for him to get out and hunt, at the same time indicating by your hand and body signal where he has to go. Providing you always remember to give the appropriate hand signal, whatever the retrieve, it will become second nature to follow this line. This mark/blind sequel should be continued until you are happy that

Jack will get out, at speed, to where you want him to hunt, without first having a mark to show him the area. As he learns, so you can increase the distances of the retrieves.

When Jack is going out happily to hunt in the area you want, it is a good plan to lay out a number of dummies, because it is imperative, as I have said, for him not to keep looking back at you for assistance. Therefore, put out about half a dozen either in a straight line, like an inverted T, or in a half moon, so that when he finds one and turns to come back to you, there can be no fear of him running across another and changing dummies, something you certainly will not want in the days ahead, when he graduates to the real thing. In due course it will be made clear how to discourage him from such sin, but at this early age just do not put temptation in his way.

As he progresses, so the training sessions will become longer, for the more he learns the more time is required to perfect what he has so far achieved, but there is a lot more yet to be learned. It should be emphasised that, however willing Jack is, you should not overdo things so that he becomes bored.

A good way to finish a training session is with a run-back. Let Jack see you drop a dummy into soft cover and walk on with him at heel. The dummy can be retrieved two ways. Having gone 15–20 yards, tell Jack to sit, then continue for a similar distance. Turn and, after a pause, give the command 'go back', together with the hand signal that you have been using from the start of training. However, to ensure that he does not get it into his head that the moment you turn he can be off, drop a dummy in front of you as you walk away from him, in such a way that he does not see it, and then, when you turn, instead of sending him back, bring him onto the dummy you have dropped. The reason for pausing is that once he catches on to what this is all about, he might get it into his head that the moment you turn and face him he can be off.

Chapter 11

Introduction to Water

When Jack is around twelve to thirteen months old he will have reached a stage when, apart for consolidating what he has already learned, if he is an apt and intelligent pupil he will be able to take in more than one lesson during his training period. In fact if you do not commence the next step in his curriculum before finalising each discipline, Jack will probably be starting to turn grey around the muzzle before you can look at him with pride and declare him a fully trained gundog.

Training is an ongoing process, one move slotting into the next in a well-ordered manner, and it should progress smoothly, providing you always remember that training is basically repetition, but progressive repetition – like a child learning arithmetic at school, addition, then subtraction, multiplication, etc. all interlinked, one unit leading into the next. Having said that, that is if you want to finish up with a good gundog, *do not cut corners and do not be in a hurry.*

Once Jack is making headway in his introduction to fur and feather, you can start introducing him to water. In human terms, Jack will now be around seven to eight years old, and many children of that age, and even much younger, love to splash through puddles. As a result they are frequently told off, but it is just the reverse with Jack. When out for a walk after heavy rain, if you spot a nice deep puddle, walk Jack, on the lead, through it and tell him what a good boy he has been. When he is happily splashing through them, then, after a good session on dummies or fur and feather, head off for your training water, providing it is a comparatively warm day. If you have any doubts about Jack entering, take a pair of thigh waders with you.

Never put a puppy on a lead and drag it in; that could well be fatal. If you have an older, more experienced dog, take it with you as a lead dog. The ideal spot to introduce Jack to water is one where he can just walk in and, if you have brought your waders

Confidence in water is essential.

you can have a paddle with him. At this stage water should be fun, an exciting new experience. If he does show any reluctance leave him sitting on the edge. Then wade in and call your older dog to you, and start to fool around and make a fuss of it. It is likely that this will be too much for young Jack and he will want to join the party, but keep him sitting until you think he is becoming almost frantic to join in, then whistle him to you.

Once he is frolicking around in the water and obviously enjoying himself, then it is time for the next step – retrieves from the shallows. Go back onto dry land, make Jack sit, then toss a dummy out so that he can retrieve it but still have the comforting feeling of being able to keep his feet on the bottom. To begin with send him within seconds of the dummy hitting the water; it is important he goes straight in on command, with no dithering about on the bank. This is a game he will undoubtedly enjoy and it will rapidly build up his confidence. Finally, for the end of the first lesson, throw a dummy so that it lands just out of his depth and he has to swim a very short distance to retrieve it. This will be the first occasion he will have had the water right over his back.

What is a dog's first natural reaction when he comes ashore after a swim? To have a good shake, of course, and when doing this he will almost certainly put down anything he might be carrying, unless he is taught not to. So right from day one, putting down a retrieve is absolutely taboo. The reason is obvious if one

Education completed. When is it my turn?

stops to think about it. On a day's shooting, a slightly wing-tipped pheasant could be dropped out into a river or lake. If your dog retrieves it, but on reaching the shore puts it down to shake, it will be away. The chances are that it will be picked again, but not always. The fact that water is involved has not changed the rules; everything has to be delivered to hand.

To avoid Jack doing what is natural, stopping and shaking, meet him right at the edge of the water, or even in the shallows to start with, giving him no chance to drop the dummy. Once you feel he is truly confident, increase the distance you throw the dummies, at the same time moving back from the bank as he becomes more experienced, but still keeping a watchful eye that he does not stop as he comes ashore to have a shake. If you have the smallest suspicion that he is going to, call or whistle him to you at once. When he is retrieving the dummies that you are throwing as far as you can out onto the water, then it's time to move onto the next phase – retrieving across water.

Much depends on what facilities you have for water training, but if you have access to a nice pond or lake, where the bottom shelves gradually away from the bank, then the following is a worthwhile exercise. Put your waders on, go down close to the water's edge, tell Jack to sit and throw a dummy straight out, away from the water. Then wade out and, when you are ready, send Jack for it so that he has to deliver it to you out in the water. Make it like just another retrieve, emphasising that there is nothing special about water, and that where you are is the point to which he retrieves. This is by no means essential to the training schedule, but it helps to strengthen the bond between you and undoubtedly Jack will find splashing back through the water to you the greatest fun. It can also be helpful when a youngster is being troublesome when coming out of water and stopping

Properly trained retrievers develop a love for water.

before delivering to hand. Bringing it back to you in the water removes the temptation to do this.

The next step is to retrieve a mark from dry land across a small stretch of water. Do not be over-ambitious to start with; distance at this stage is of little importance. What you are aiming for is a quick entry, swimming *straight across* and, most important, an easy entrance and exit to the water. More difficult banks can be added to the training programme once Jack realises that the command 'get over' means exactly that. It is therefore wise to stand close to the water's edge to begin with, so as to make sure he goes directly over. There is nothing more infuriating, on a day's shooting, than to drop a bird across a quite narrow stretch of water and send your dog with the command 'get over' only for it to start hunting about on the near bank. So from day one 'over' must mean just that. Just in case there is any hesitation, a stone or two in your pocket which you can lob over onto the far bank as encouragement will not come amiss. It is always a good idea to anticipate a problem when training, rather than get caught unprepared if it occurs. The chances are that if you have played your part correctly it will not, but better safe than sorry.

Once Jack is retrieving from across water, then it is a matter of progression – longer distances and more difficult entries and exits. This is also the time to give Jack a chance to show you how bold he is by taking him somewhere with a near-vertical bank, throwing a dummy and encouraging him to jump in. Just a word of warning: make sure that having jumped in and collected the dummy, there is somewhere where he can get back onto dry land.

Once Jack is crossing water for marks, then the fewer retrieves he has actually from water the better, at least for the time being. If dogs will swim out into a river or lake, then they will retrieve a bird that is floating on the water. The final stage in water training is for a blind from across the other side of a stream, river or lake. This slots in with what has been dealt with in Chapter 10, hunting for and retrieving blinds, which you will be working on before Jack has finished his water training. Incidentally, try and find several different places where you can send him across for marks. You do not want to get it into his head that there is only one place where he swims. When the time comes, take him to the place where he has been regularly swimming across for a mark, but this time put out a blind before sending him. It all comes down to instilling into Jack's head that 'get over' means precisely that, irrespective of whether he has seen anything or not.

Chapter 12

Taking a Runner

There are few shooting people who would dispute that the paramount requirement of any Gun's dog is picking runners. To oversimplify the matter, if push came to shove anything else could be picked by hand, even if it meant bashing one's way through heavy briars or swimming out into a lake or across a river. This may seem ridiculous but it is certainly possible and has, on at least two occasions, been known to happen. In one instance it led to the start of what was to become quite a well-known kennel of Labradors in the fifties and sixties. A British Army major who had served many years in India was a keen shot and, with his brother officers, annually shot various *biels* – large flooded areas, much favoured by vast numbers of duck following the monsoon. The major's wife, a keen swimmer, used to accompany him and swim for the duck he shot, acting as his retriever. He inherited the family estate, which included an extensive area of marshland criss-crossed by a number of small rivers and streams, providing excellent duck and snipe shooting. The major retired from the Army and moved to the family home. When the duck season started, the weather was warm and so the wife quite happily continued as she had in India and readily acted as her husband's retriever. By mid-October, conditions had changed and the lady went on strike and bought a trained Labrador bitch, providing the foundation for her kennel, which in due course produced a number of field trial winners. But the one thing a Gun cannot do for himself (and nor can his wife) is pick a runner.

Amusing though this anecdote may be, generally gundogs are trained to do this work, just as Jack watching his boss bash his way into dense cover to pick a dead bird is not on the training curriculum. So, before you move onto training to pick runners, test Jack in heavy cover such as briars, with either a mark on a dummy or, to make it more worthwhile from Jack's point of view, a cold pheasant or partridge, even a duck. It is unlikely that you will have any problem if you have adhered to the selection and training programme outlined in previous chapters.

Like all other facets that combine in making a good working gundog, scenting ability varies from dog to dog, and from knowledge gleaned over many years from foxhounds, it has been shown to be an inherited factor. Further, it is a fact that the Golden Retrievers have excellent scenting powers and will take an 'air scent', so that they frequently come into their own on a bad scenting day. If you have heeded the advice given in Chapter 2 and Jack has come from a litter whose dam is noted for her game-finding ability, then you have done all that you can in this connection. It is now up to you to develop what inherited talent he may have.

One very famous trainer, when asked how he taught a dog to use its nose and pick runners, retorted: 'Work. If they've anything about them they'll teach themselves.' This is true, but whatever natural ability Jack may have can be developed. This was touched on in Chapter 10, when we discussed getting him to use his nose to seek out a dummy or cold game, but then Jack saw you walking around as he sat impatiently waiting to see what happened. Whilst dogs do not reason, hopefully he had enough nous to realise that something was afoot when you were walking about out in front of him. Now comes the stage where you send him out to an area to hunt where he has seen nothing. His job is to find and follow an unbroken line of scent.

This raises the question of what you are going to scent a dummy with. Aniseed, as used by drag hunts, certainly leaves a strong and pungent scent, is easy to follow and teaches a dog to 'take a line', but I do not recommend it unless you are really pushed for something with which to scent your dummies. So much depends on your circumstances and, indeed, the time of year. In the past it was simple enough: a wing-clipped mallard waddling off through light reeds, grass, corn or roots was ideal. One professional trainer, some years ago, had several very domesticated wing-clipped mallard which he taught to lead. A duck leaves a great scent. This trainer was also a keen fisherman. He had a helper who would take one of the ducks to lay a trail, leading it on the end of a fishing rod and line. The line would be attached to a ferret collar around the duck's neck. With the aid of these it was possible to take the duck for a walk and still keep 40–50 feet away from it. When the duck had gone the required distance, the helper moved round in front of it, being careful not

Drive in post at C, or whatever you are going to pass the line around and walk to A. Do not cross the line from C to B, thus ensuring you do not leave your scent. Then attach whatever you intend to use to lay the line and toss it across to B. Then pull the *retrieve* slowly along the ground towards C. If you use a doubled length of line then, rather than having it trailing along behind Jack, you can release one end and draw it back to you, leaving whatever is to be retrieved free of any encumbrance. If using game an *eye* can be made with a loop of string around the bird's neck to pass the line through and, normally, there is one already in a dummy.

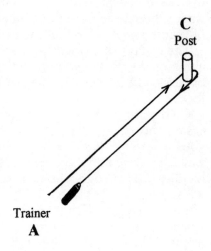

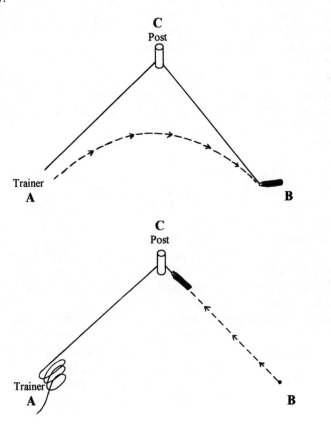

to cross its line, picked it up and left either a dummy or cold game where the line ended. The trainer would then appear with his dog, and send it out to hunt, and he was nearly always successful.

These days this would probably be severely frowned upon, although the ducks certainly did not worry. Moreover, it is a lot of hassle just to train one dog, so we will find a simpler way for Jack.

Cold game such as a partridge or teal is ideal, providing the easiest way of laying a line. The knack is how to do this so that you are sure Jack is following the game's scent and not yours. One way is to drive into the ground a thin iron bar or an old broom handle, sharpened to a point so that it goes in easily; make sure it is smooth so that a line will slip round it easily and with no fear of getting caught. If you are lucky there may be a convenient fencing post, or even a sapling which will meet your requirements. Take a length of light fishing line, or, if you are unable to obtain this, green garden string. Pass it around the post, which becomes the apex of an equilateral triangle, point C in the diagram. Taking a double length of the line back to the base line of the triangle, point A, attach your partridge or teal to one end and throw it as far across towards B as you can; then drag it up towards C. To begin with 15–18 yards is ample. It should be through short grass or corn, just enough to hide the retrieve. Drop your end of the line and fetch Jack as quickly as possible from where he has been waiting. Do not be long in getting him and sending him out to the 'fall'. If he follows the scent you have laid, it is most important that the line attached to whatever you are using is light enough not to slow or impede Jack's return in any way when he is galloping back with his find.

Another way of laying a line, should you happen to be a fisherman, is to take a good strong casting rod, attach a teal or partridge to the end of the line, then cast it downwind, to the point from where you intend sending Jack. Let the retrieve lie where it has fallen for a few moments, before slowly reeling it in, untie the lure, leaving it free for Jack to retrieve, having worked the scent you have left into the wind.

There are a number of ways to teach Jack to use his nose. One, pictured in one of the older books on training, shows two men with a long cord running through a small loop of string around a pheasant's neck. They are shown walking 40–50 yards apart, slowly dragging the pheasant along the ground between them. Having gone the desired distance, even zigzagging a little bit as they go providing it is always mainly into the wind, one drops his end of the cord and the other pulls it in through the loop, leaving the pheasant free of any encumbrance.

Laying a trail for Jack to follow provides scope for all kinds of ingenuity. Your aim, of course, is that he should eventually only follow a blood scent – unless he is destined to both hunt and flush game, but that is not what this book is really about. When Jack has faith in his nose and you visualise him picking strong runners 80–100 yards from where they fell, then this could be the time to enlist the help of a youngster with a mountain bike. Attach the retrieve to a length of cord. Give the end to your young assistant with instructions to ride off across stubble, rough grass, or whatever may be available, to a predetermined spot. Then tell him or her to gather it up, drop the retrieve and pedal off out of the area, leaving it clear for Jack to work the line and proudly bring his find to hand. If he does it is likely that he will not be the only one feeling proud.

Now to the question of how to leave a blood scent. As I said earlier, so much depends on your circumstances and where you live. If you live in the country and have access to land around you, where you can take your gun and shoot a pigeon, that greatly decreases the problem. A little prior organisation is required so that your young cycling helper is standing by to set off immediately you are ready, but impress upon him or her to go slowly – you are aiming to leave a strong blood scent. First shoot a woodpigeon. What usually happens when you particularly want one there is never one around, but you will eventually be successful. Whilst it is still hot cut open the breast and make it as bloody as possible. *Under no circumstances leave it for Jack to retrieve.* Rub it over a dummy before your young helper sets off. If it is impossible to shoot a pigeon an alternative is a rabbit, but it is much better not to use this except as a last resort, for, at this stage, you should do as little as possible to encourage Jack's natural interest in rabbits – a frequent cause of much original sin in all gundogs. However, if it is the only option open to you, then gut the rabbit as soon as you have shot it, making it as bloody as possible. Again do not leave it for Jack. Then the procedure is just the same as with a pigeon.

Should you be fortunate enough to live in the vicinity of a shoot which rears a large number of pheasants, the chances are that a quiet drive around roads adjoining coverts where there are release pens will yield just what you need – a pheasant that has been hit by a car will nearly always be easy to come by. Occasionally a bird can be found that has not been too knocked about, which could be left as a retrieve after Jack has followed the scent. If you do happen to have such a shoot close by, you will more than likely know the gamekeeper, but if you do not, make a point of getting to know him. However good a keeper he is, he will lose poults when he puts them out in the release pens. Such casualties could be very useful for you when working on cold game and, undoubtedly, Jack will like them an awful lot more than dummies!

Before leaving the all-important matter of teaching Jack to use his nose, so far concentrated on feathered retrieves, which form the group of smells to which you have been activating his subconscious to respond, there is one point I should mention. It is surprising how frequently a shot hare can bring about the downfall of a dog which, up to this point, has been running a good trial. Whilst Jack's future may not be in field trialling, it is important that he finds and quickly retrieves any hares added to the bag on a day's shooting. A blood scent is not the only one you should acquaint Jack with, for it seems, at times, that a shot hare can give off virtually none.

However, powder and shot leave a very pungent scent and this is something Jack should be introduced to and taught that it means there is a retrieve to be found. To achieve this, prior to taking Jack out training, drop a dummy as close to a tall seeded sugar beet as you can. Then break the top over to mark where it is. This method of marking is preferable to tying a white strip of rag onto the beet, something an intelligent dog will quickly cotton on to. Then, with your lad at heel, shoot the 'marker' beet and send him quickly into the area, where there will be a strong smell of shot. As in the case of all exercise, don't look for distance to start with, this is not important. In fact it doesn't matter whether Jack marks where you shot to begin with. The whole object of the exercise is to equate the smell of powder and shot with a retrieve. You can lengthen this exercise until you have a friend shooting a beet a hundred yards or more away. There will be those who will say 'Oh, I haven't access to sugar beet.' The answer is that any rough cover will do, as long as it hides the dummy, for it does not require great ingenuity to construct a marker.

Chapter 13

Long Retrieves –
the Dummy Launcher

To date virtually all the work Jack has done has been within the distance that you can throw a dummy – except for run-backs and the few occasions you have had a friend with you to throw marks, but even these have only been 35–40 yards. Not all birds fall within such a distance of your peg on a day's shooting, so it is important that Jack learns to mark a fall much further away. Your greatest aid here is a dummy launcher. In simple terms, this is a short tube which forms a barrel, about 4¼ in in length, and takes a .22 blank cartridge. Approximately ¾ in from the end there is a rubber ring seal to retain maximum pressure. A launcher dummy has a tight-fitting cylindrical centre that slides over the tube, down to a hinged base which gives access for loading. The dummy is fired by means of the .22 blank. The whole is mounted on a recoil handle and, according to the elevation, will fire a dummy 100–120 yards. Like all training equipment it is obtainable from Turner Richards. Two types of dummy are available: plastic or green canvas. I prefer the latter because the dog is used to the feel of canvas after the dummies he has been retrieving.

Before you actually use the launcher, let Jack sniff the dummy, for it will be a strange scent, mainly gunpowder. Having done this, sit him down as usual and throw a launcher dummy for him to retrieve. Then go to some clear ground and slide the dummy about halfway onto the tube; this gives a short retrieve with which to start. If there is no problem – and it is most unlikely there will be – then fire a dummy the full distance.

As soon as he is on his way throw out several dummies so that they fall 8–10 yards on either side of his return route, where he can see them. At this stage of his training it is very unlikely that he will try to switch retrieves, but the recurring theme throughout his education is that it is better to avoid trouble than have to correct it. But be on your toes, ready to 'rush out roaring' as one very famous trainer was fond of saying, for dummy launchers will frequently make a dog excited. Should Jack fall from grace, grab him and give him a good shake. Then give him the launcher dummy, making him carry it back to where you were standing. Collect the hand dummies and go through the same procedure again, and woe betide Jack if he errs again. If you have played your part correctly, however, he should not do so. If he has to be corrected, make it a one-off occurrence.

Having reached the stage where Jack will return through a positive minefield of dummies, try one more diversion. As he nears you throw out a dummy to the side of his line of return. He may look, but that is all he may do and, indeed, it is all he should do.

Dummy launchers tend to excite a dog, so it is advisable to use them sparingly. However, having got Jack accustomed to the launcher, it can be of considerable help in certain aspects of training, particularly for firing a dummy across water into cover. This also applies to putting a blind out into long rough grass or set-aside. When you have done this two or three times it is a good idea to drop a dummy as you are walking along, unseen by Jack, and, having fired the launcher, send him back for the 'blind' behind you. Then, when he has got this, send him for the one from the launcher. The point of this is that Jack must not start to think every bang means a retrieve out in front of him. Another useful ploy in developing total steadiness is to sit Jack down on clear ground, where he has a good view of all that is happening, then walk on and fire a couple of dummies from the launcher back behind him. Drop a dummy where you are standing whilst Jack is watching the ones from the launcher. Return to him, continuing with him at heel to within a short distance of the launcher dummies. Leave him sitting whilst you collect them, then send him for the one you dropped.

One other exercise for which a launcher can be useful is to fire a dummy over a belt of trees so that you can train Jack to go right through cover and hunt beyond it. His natural instinct, particularly after your training, will be to hunt in the cover, but it is sometimes very useful to be able to send a dog into cover and on out the far side. If you decide to do this, try and find a belt to start with which is not too wide and where you are able to see Jack. Then you can stop him on the whistle if he tries to hunt the cover and push him through to the far side. If you attempt this, it is advisable, to begin with at least, to find a place where the dummy will land on clear ground.

Dummy launchers are a useful tool in training, provided they are not over-used; if they are they can easily excite a dog and undo months of hard work. To vary the retrieve and make it possibly more interesting for Jack, you can cover a dummy with rabbit skin, but it will not go quite as far as a normal dummy. Incidentally, one can get stronger cartridges than those normally supplied, and these will fire a dummy for the better part of 200 yards. But one word of warning: if you decide to use these make sure you are holding the launcher tightly – they have a real kick to them.

Chapter 14

Steadiness to Fur and Live Game

Steadiness is something that has been developed throughout Jack's training, for he has had to learn to disregard the various diversion to which he has been subjected during his weeks of schooling. However, dummies being thrown across his path when returning with a retrieve, or a fur-covered one, attached to a strong length of elastic whipping across in front of him at a speed that any living rabbit would envy, are no match for the real thing. Again so much depends on your circumstances. If you live in the heart of the country where rabbits abound, then Jack will hopefully have learned from an early age that they are absolutely taboo. From the first time he sees one, you should blow the stop whistle and, at the same time tell him, very firmly, '*no*'. If he makes even the slightest move towards one, grab him and unceremoniously put him back where he should have remained, making it very clear that they are not for him until you indicate differently.

Nevertheless as an added safeguard it is a good idea to put temptation in his way and ensure that he knows that chasing rabbits is not for him. One way of doing this is to take a fresh rabbit skin, leaving the head on to make it a bit more realistic, attach it to a light line and put it out in grass just tall enough to cover it until it moves. Lay the line out so that it crosses a piece of an old branch 4–6 in in diameter. Then fetch Jack, sit him, downwind, close to the branch and just a few yards from where the line runs; move to the end and start to pull the 'rabbit' in. Just before it reaches the branch give it a quick jerk and it should realistically 'jump' up over it. If Jack views it with disdain, you have done your job well. If he does not and makes a dive for it, then by now you should know what to do.

Some professional trainers have pens where they keep rabbits, frequently wild ones they have caught or acquired from a friendly gamekeeper. If there is a pen close to you try and get permission to take Jack along. There is no standard size, they are normally about 20–30 yards long and about half that wide. Such pens are usually well stocked, and there are always plenty of escape pipes, arcs and stick heaps, if some invader to the rabbits' territory does not conform to the correct code of conduct.

If you are fortunate enough to obtain access to a pen, have Jack on a choke-chain when you first take him in. If he deviates as much as an inch from his normal heeling position when you put up a rabbit, give a sharp jerk on the chain and an equally sharp '*no*'. When he is walking around the pen at heel, on a completely loose lead, giving the impression that you may be seeing rabbits, but he certainly is not, then it is time for the next move. Have him on a check cord and throw a dummy within a few feet of a rabbit; they become very blasé about dogs invading their space, and the chances are that it will not run away. Send Jack for the dummy, letting the cord run through your hand in case, horror of horrors, he thinks the rabbit is more interesting than the dummy. In that way you can bring him up very short, be out to him in a flash and let him know that you are not pleased. This might happen a couple of times before he realises that the best policy is to turn a blind eye to these forbidden attractions. If the owner of the pen can spare a few minutes, it is helpful if he drives some of the rabbits past you whilst you stand with Jack sitting beside you off the lead. But be on your toes, just in case. Owners of rabbit pens do not take kindly to having the inmates grabbed by some undisciplined dog, and it could be costly.

If this routine goes well the next step is to have Jack outside the pen, throw a dummy in amongst the rabbits and send him for it. Providing you have taken enough time and sufficient steps to ensure that rabbits no longer tempt him, this should cause no problem. The final 'passing out test' is to put one or two blinds in the pen, fetch Jack and work him for these from some 20 or so yards outside the enclosure. This can always be a tense moment, so if you even momentarily think Jack is going to succumb to temptation, blow 'stop' on your whistle, move up to the edge of the pen and handle him onto the dummies from there. Once this is achieved you have done all you can and Jack should ignore fur except when sent for it.

Feather is a bit more of a poser, because you can only educate Jack to ignore unshot game, that is game that is not carrying a blood scent, if you can find somewhere that you can walk him through pheasants and, where possible, partridges. Years ago one or two trainers had pens with pinioned pheasants in them, similar to a rabbit pen, but very few, if any, do these days. If you can take Jack out on shoots and walk with the beaters, with him at heel off the lead, this gives a great opportunity for you to impress upon him that pheasants which fly are no concern of his. Every time a pheasant gets up anywhere near you, a firm 'no' should quickly get the message across to him. When he has gained a little experience actually working as a gundog, he will quickly accept that if a bird is not carrying a blood scent then it is not the one he is after.

Chapter 15

The Moment of Truth

The time has come to find out how good a trainer you have been and how receptive Jack has been as a pupil. Earlier I said that woodpigeons were unsuitable for training, but now a stage has been reached when they can play a vital part in putting the finishing touches to all your months of careful work. If you have access to a wood where pigeons come in to roost, take Jack, your gun and a pocketful of cartridges, and go and wait for their arrival. Sit Jack up about 10–15 yards away from where you are going to stand and then wait. This also familiarises Jack to the fact, that unlike training on dummies, there can be long waits when doing the real thing and he has to sit still until he gets his cue to join in.

Pick the first pigeon you shoot by hand, at the same time keeping an eye on Jack; pigeons falling out of the sky and fluttering on the ground are vastly more exciting than canvas dummies. There is one exception: if the first pigeon you shoot falls away behind Jack and you are pretty certain he has marked it, then let him have it and give the command 'go back' and the appropriate signal. When he has delivered it to hand make sure you immediately clean his mouth of feathers, then sit him back where he was. If you give Jack the first bird, pick the next bird or two yourself, but let him have one more before you head for home. However well the woodies are coming in, do not get carried away; you are there to train Jack, not for an evening's shooting. If the opportunity is there you can repeat this a couple of times a week and, after a few evenings, shoot more, but pick all the ones laying around where Jack can see them, leaving those that have dropped in cover for him to find and retrieve.

Having got Jack acclimatised to being shot over and are confident that he is steady, leaving you to concentrate on your shooting, then you have achieved your objective – nearly. Do not, at this late stage, spoil the ship for a ha'p'orth of tar; do not rush Jack. If you are in the fortunate position of being involved in a shoot with reasonably large bags, the chances are you will know someone who is similarly placed. If you do, ask if you may take Jack along for a day, purely as a spectator. Stand well back, and, keeping Jack on the lead, let him watch. After the first drive have him still sitting, but off the lead. Whilst he is watching, make sure that you are also watching him and be prepared to reprimand him if you think he is about to run in. This first day out on a shoot is purely a sightseeing tour for Jack – not even one retrieve. The next time you take him to a shoot, go and stand in the line between two Guns who preferably have no dogs with them. When the drive is over let Jack have a retrieve; it does not matter what, as long as it's dead and lying in the open. Then leave him sitting and pick any more around your area by hand. Repeat this for a couple more drives, then for the fourth one go and stand with a Gun, providing he or she does not mind and has not got a dog. At the end of the drive, if the Gun has several birds down, pick the nearest ones yourself and send Jack for the one furthest away; you may have to handle him onto it. One word of warning: do not send him if you see some other dog or dogs homing in on the bird you have selected; at this stage you do not want Jack joining in the general hoovering up that frequently follows a drive on many shoots. Better he sits and watches than starts competing for the birds to be picked.

During these informative and, for Jack, very exciting times you would be well advised not to be a Gun until he has had two or three days out with your full and undivided attention, and you are sure he is rock steady. Always sit him with his back to the drive when you do start to shoot over him, so that he can mark what falls behind you. When you do start, sit him a good 6–8 yards out in front of you. If you want to keep him steady never send for a bird whilst the drive is going on and, even more important looking to the future, *never* send him for a runner in the open during his first season, for that then becomes a course which will undoubtedly excite Jack and could easily undo all your good work. Let him watch them run off, until, once again, the unusual becomes the usual. Quite frequently, if you are in the line as a Gun, you will find that some hosts do not approve of your dog being worked whilst a drive is going on. There is no reason why, after a few outings, you should not hunt Jack through cover, or along a ditch from the place where you saw a runner disappear from view, but then he will largely be hunting by scent, not sight.

Up to Christmas one day a week will be ample for Jack to be

out on a shoot. During January twice a week will be fine, but no more. If he is rock steady, retrieving dead or live birds from cover on the last day of the season, then you indeed have a dog for your game.

To some this may seem to have been a long-winded training course, but the aim has been to get as near to perfection as the material you have been working on will provide. Remember that, with luck, Jack will be your friend and shooting companion for many seasons to come, so the outcome should be worth all the work you have put into his training.

Chapter 16

So, the Shooting Season is Over

Come the first week of February there are many people, throughout the country, who are suffering from withdrawal symptoms, be it from shooting or dog handling, and whether the latter is picking up or field trialling, they can be equally compelling and absorbing.

If you are amongst these, give a thought to Jack. He too will be missing the pleasures of his days out with the gun. If he has lived up to your hopes and expectations, then it is more than possible that, at some time during the shooting season, you may have had daydreams about working tests and field trials, as Jack has taken the line of a runner, disappeared from view and then come racing back with his quarry. At that moment you may be forgiven for thinking 'Was there ever such a dog?'

If the possibility of running in working tests becomes a truly serious thought, still stick to what has been the theme throughout this book: do not rush things if you intend to win, as opposed to having a jolly day out with Jack. Go and watch a few working tests, talk to people, watch and learn. Unless you have done an ultra-super job training Jack, the chances are that you will see that the top dogs in tests are sharper on the whistle and are looking for more pinpoint directions than you have been giving Jack during the shooting season, when you have simply guided him into an area and then left him to get on with his job. You can sharpen him up on this, but do not forget that next shooting season you will expect him to go about his business without constant handling. If the idea of tests appeals, by all means have a go once you have been to a few to see what it is all about. There is normally a good sense of camaraderie, Jack will enjoy running in them, and if you keep your eyes and ears open you will undoubtedly increase your knowledge of training. Incidentally, when you attend as a spectator leave Jack at home, as unentered dogs are not encouraged, and at field trials under KC regulations, they are barred.

Much the same applies to field trialling. If you have a yen to try your luck with Jack, go and watch, talk to people with experience and learn the whys and wherefores of trialling. Find out why a dog you thought had done well only finished up with a Certificate of Merit. It could be one or a combination of several factors, such as an awkward pick-up, poor delivery, too much handling on just one particular bird and so forth. Weigh up all these aspects before becoming involved, for once 'bitten' you will find trialling could well bring to light a zest for competition that you never knew you had before. If you have done the ground-work for producing a good shooting dog, then it is not too

The only five dogs of workable age in my kennel at the end of the shooting season 1998/99 when this book was first conceived. They were:– **Back, left to right,** FT Ch Lafayette Tolley, Loughbrook Gold Charm of Lafayette. **Front, left to right,** Canburne Fennel of Lafayette, Deep Barley Ross of Lafayette, Strammers Honey of Lafayette.

difficult, providing Jack has the talent, to augment this to make him worth running in trials.

Whether you become involved in the competitive side of gundog work or not, do not let Jack 'go to seed' during the off-season. A couple of times a week, work him on dummies; it will help keep him (and possibly you) fit. As the start of the new shooting season approaches give him plenty of exercise. Try long retrieves from the dummy launcher, but be careful not to do so many that it hots him up. Long run-backs and equally long 'sit and stays' – when you leave him and walk 150 or so yards before whistling him up – will also help. Years ago one could get on a bike and take one's dogs off around country roads to get them fit and harden their pads. There is no doubt that road work does this and is a benefit to a dog when asked to face really tough briars and similar cover.

To close, I can do no better than to borrow and paraphrase the words of that great author on field sports in the early part of the last century, namely Patrick Chalmers: 'And now that my fun is finished, I'll make bold to hope that some may find and have some fun from accepting and practising my facts and will say tolerantly of my fancies, "Why, of course it may well be so." Of one thing I am certain: you will never know unless you try!'

Appendix I
Conditions of Sale

I, the Buyer, ... agree to purchase the . . . .
puppy, Kennel Club Registration Number . . . . from
the Seller for the sum of £ . . . . . . The Buyer, having examined
certificates in respect of Hereditary Eye Diseases, Hip Dysplasia and
other such documents as may be available applicable to the parents of
the above puppy, as issued by a qualified veterinary surgeon, accepts
that such certificates do not in any way constitute a Warranty, but are
purely an opinion given at the time of examination by the veterinary
surgeon, as the said puppy, being a living creature, cannot carry a
guarantee that could be applicable to an inanimate object. The Seller
undertakes that the puppy, at the time of sale is in good health and corre-
sponds to the description as given by the Seller and that all other
warranties, conditions or terms relating to the puppy, whether implied
by statute or common law or otherwise are excluded.

The Seller agrees that, on being notified of any problem, the Buyer may
return the puppy within one calendar month from the date of purchase,
providing the Buyer presents a veterinary surgeon's certificate stating
that the puppy was suffering from a condition that was to its detriment
at the time of purchase. Given such circumstances the Seller will be
responsible for the veterinary surgeon's fee.

Notwithstanding this Condition of Sale the Seller's liability to the Buyer,
whether for any breach of the Condition of Sale or otherwise, shall not
in any event exceed the Price and the Seller shall be under no liability
for any direct loss and/or expense or indirect loss and/or expense
suffered by the Buyer or the liability to third parties incurred by the
Buyer.

Signature of Buyer . . . . Date . . . .

Address . . . .

. . . .

Signature of Seller . . . . Date . . . .

Address . . . .

. . . .

Appendix II

Roger Skinner Ltd,
The Mills,
Stradbroke,
Eye,
Suffolk,
IP21 5HL   Tel. 01 379 384 247

Appendix III

Turner Richards,
Cardigan Street,
Birmingham,
B4 7SA   Tel. 01 213 595 577